Natural
Wonders
—— *of* ——
Massachusetts

Natural
Wonders
of
Massachusetts

A Guide to
Parks, Preserves
& Wild Places

Nancy Prajzner

Illustrated by Harriet Corbett

Country Roads Press
C A S T I N E • M A I N E

Natural Wonders of Massachusetts

Published by Country Roads Press
P.O. Box 286, Lower Main Street
Castine, Maine 04421

Text and cover design by Studio 3.
Cover photograph © Kindra Clineff 1994.
Illustrations by Harriet Corbett.
Typesetting by Typeworks.

ISBN 1-56626-108-2

Library of Congress Cataloging-in-Publication Data

Prajzner, Nancy.
    Natural wonders of Massachusetts / author, Nancy Prajzner ;
illustrator, Harriet Corbett.
        p.   cm.
    Includes bibliographical references (p. 124) and index.
    ISBN 1-56626-108-2 : $9.95
    1. Massachusetts – Guidebooks.   2. Natural history –
Massachusetts – Guidebooks.   3. Natural areas – Massachusetts –
Guidebooks.   4. Parks – Massachusetts – Guidebooks.
    5. Botanical gardens – Massachusetts – Guidebooks.   I. Title.
F62.3.P73   1994
917.4404′43 – dc20   94-18860
                                                                      CIP

Printed in the United States of America.
10 9 8 7 6 5 4 3 2 1

To my Mother

Contents

Introduction

I was standing atop Quabbin Hill when I saw a few faint streaks of color in the distance to the northeast. It was the beginning of a rainbow.

The entire arch of color formed as I stood watching. Just as gradually the color dissipated, but only for a few moments. Soon light rays formed a second colorful, arch.

The rainbow made me realize what wonders nature offers. They often are nearby. The unspoiled Quabbin Reservoir in Belchertown is just twenty minutes from my home. In winter I might see a majestic eagle soar above its waters.

Massachusetts packs a lot of wonderful sights in just 8,284 square miles. In my outings across the Bay State I walked pristine beaches on Cape Cod, went deep into an Atlantic white cedar swamp, smelled the fragrances of wildflowers, and climbed to the summit of 3,491-foot Mount Greylock in the Berkshires.

Besides eagles at Quabbin, I saw humpback whales in the Atlantic Ocean, harbor seals on winter beaches at the Cape, and white-tailed deer in the forests of central and western Massachusetts.

It was a wonderful endeavor. Many times I felt as though I had reached the pot of gold at the end of the rainbow.

Many people along the way contributed to my learning experiences, particularly members of the Massachusetts Division of Parks and Forests, Massachusetts Trustees of Reservations, Metropolitan District Commission, Cape Cod National Seashore, and Massachusetts Audubon Society. I owe them all a thank-you.

Just as helpful were the ardent birdwatchers I met at Mount Tom Reservation, Quabbin Reservoir, and Parker River National Wildlife Refuge. They readily shared their viewing scopes and expert knowledge. They gladly pointed out red-shouldered hawks, American kestrels, and crossbills.

A note on walking trails in Massachusetts. Raccoon rabies has been increasing. Rabies is spread through a bite or scratch from an infected animal. Do not feed wild animals or approach them.

Always inspect for ticks after a hike. Deer ticks cause Lyme disease, a debilitating illness if it is not detected and treated early.

1

Western Massachusetts

SAGE'S RAVINE

My decision to visit Sage's Ravine late in the year was rewarded when a white-tailed deer bolted across the trail twenty yards ahead of me. I'm not sure who was startled more.

I had put off my visit until early December in the hope that I could sit undisturbed and listen to Sage's Ravine Brook as it danced over the rocks and raced through the mile-long gully in the bucolic town of Mount Washington. That's not always possible during summer and early fall, the two prime hiking seasons in Massachusetts.

Areas posted with signs warning visitors to keep off

1

eroded banks attest to the popularity of the ravine, which is accessible only on foot. The Appalachian Trail passes through the ravine, bringing hordes of casual hikers, and in August, through-hikers on their journey from Georgia to Maine.

On the brook's north side sits a camping area that is a highly sought-after destination for an overnight stay. The Appalachian Mountain Club maintains the campground, which contains ten sites, some with tent platforms.

Carved out by Sage's Ravine Brook, the ravine is wild and beautiful. The brook is clear and cold. It was swollen from the previous day's sleet and snow when I visited.

The white-blazed Appalachian Trail follows a narrow, slippery path between the brook and the steep, rock-strewn southern slope. Yellow birch, red maple, and eastern hemlock cling to the hillside, which ferns carpet in places. American beech and mountain laurel dominate the sunnier and drier opposite side.

Sage's Ravine Brook descends roughly 400 feet before it leaves the ravine. More beauty awaits as Bear Rock Falls lies one and a half miles to the north.

Where: Take Massachusetts Turnpike to exit 2 in Lee. Take State 183 south to Stockbridge and then State 7 south to Great Barrington. Turn right onto State 41 and follow Egremont signs to the junction of State 23. Turn right onto Mount Washington Road, which becomes East Street in the town of Mount Washington. Road becomes gravel just south of Mount Washington State Forest headquarters. Follow for another three miles. The small parking area is on the left just before the road ends.

Follow a blue-blazed trail spur for twenty minutes until it reaches the white-blazed Appalachian Trail (AT). Turn left on the AT. Reach Sage's Ravine in a quarter mile.

Best time to visit: Summer and fall. Early spring is mud season. The ravine is beautiful in winter when waterfalls are frozen, but walking is difficult in icy conditions. The road to the trailhead might be impassable.

An alternate route is to take the Under Mountain Trail. It begins off State 41 just over the border in Connecticut. It connects with the AT and runs approximately four miles to Sage's Ravine. You can shorten the distance by taking Paradise Lane Trail rather than the AT over Bear Mountain.

Activities: Hiking, camping, snowshoeing.

Other: Heading north, the Appalachian Trail reaches the short side trail to Bear Rock Falls and then climbs the summits of Mount Race (2,365 feet) and Mount Everett (2,602 feet). Just before the steep climb up Mount Everett, the Race Brook Falls Trail enters from the right. It's worth a side trip in high-water times during spring and fall. It's a series of five beautiful falls. It's also reached from a trail off State 41.

Heading south on the Appalachian Trail leads to the summit of Bear Mountain (2,316 feet) in neighboring Connecticut. It's the highest mountain in Connecticut.

For more information:

Appalachian Mountain Club, Berkshire Chapter, P.O. Box 1800, Lanesborough, MA 01237; 413-443-0011.

BASH BISH FALLS

Cascading 1,000 feet through a series of gorges and finally plummeting eighty feet into a sparkling pool, Bash Bish Falls is the most spectacular waterfall in western Massachusetts.

Its waters begin in a nondescript spring high in Mount Washington State Forest. Bash Bish Brook gains speed and volume as it journeys downward. The water's force is best displayed at the top of the falls, where it rushes over the edge with a deafening roar. A granite outcropping divides the last section of the falls into two, fifty-foot cataracts.

Below the pool Bash Bish Brook continues downward into neighboring New York and Taconic State Park.

There is a different beauty and charm to the falls each season. Spring brings the greatest flow of water as snow melt from surrounding mountains — Alander Mountain (2,239 feet) and Bash Bish Mountain (1,890) are the two highest — swell Bash Bish Brook and Bash Brook Falls. It's one of my favorite places to usher in spring.

The second largest volume of water occurs in fall. It's also when foliage of red oak, sugar maples, and yellow birches frames the falls. Water flow is greatly reduced in summer, except for the quick rush after rainstorms. Aster and goldenrod in full bloom in surrounding woods try their best to make up for the diminished falls.

Winter turns Bash Bish into a wonderland of ice.

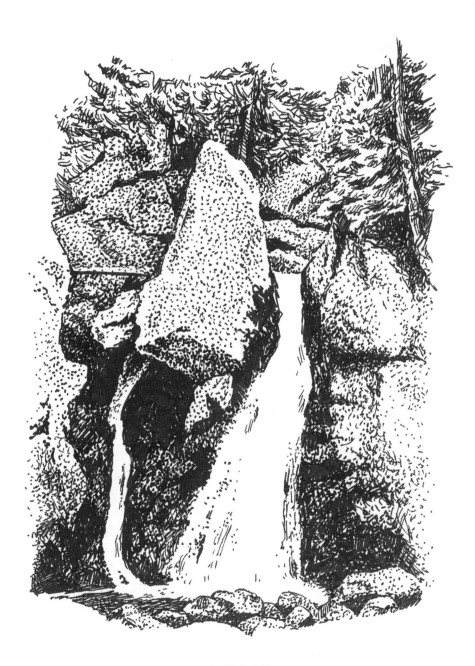

Bash Bish Falls

Frozen spray coats the rocks and forms ice sculptures.

Like most New England streams, Bash Bish Brook was created during the melting of the last glacier, which covered the region 10,000 to 20,000 years ago. During the glacier's retreat it scraped up sediment that blocked streambeds. Waterfalls, like Bash Bish, were formed when the blocked streams broke through and the waters rushed down mountains, often following joints or weak points in the rock. Sediment in the water continues to erode the streambed today. A short trail leads from the parking lot to the top of the falls and offers a view westward to the New York countryside. A steel-cabled fence runs along the edge of the cliffs.

Another trail leads down to the pool below the falls. It's a popular spot for enjoying a cool spray and taking photographs.

The surrounding 4,500-acre Mount Washington State Forest contains thirty miles of trails. The most strenuous is a five-mile hike that starts at forest headquarters and climbs over Alander and Bash Bish Mountains. The ridge line affords sweeping views as far west as the Catskills.

Sometimes the attraction is closer. My approach made an excited chipmunk dive into a ground hole on the trail's edge. I soon wished for a hole of my own to dive into when a driving rain began to fall. I was still two miles from my tent site at the Mount Washington camping area.

Another choice for hikers is a state-owned cabin between the north and south peaks of Alander Mountain.

Just a mile north from the forest headquarters is

Mount Everett State Reservation with its picturesque Guilder Pond. One can hike 5.5 miles of the Appalachian Trail to Mount Everett or take the gravel auto road that ends less than a half-mile from the top.

Mount Everett, at 2,606 feet, is the highest peak south of Mount Greylock in the Berkshires. It offers wonderful views in all directions.

Where: Bash Bish Falls is on Falls Road off East Street in Mount Washington. To reach Mount Everett State Reservation and Mount Washington State Forest, continue south on East Street.

Best time to visit: Water volume is highest in spring.

Hours: Falls area is open dawn to dusk. Gate to Mount Everett Road opens 10:00 A.M. to 6:00 P.M. May through October.

Activities: Hiking, camping ($5 at state forest primitive sites, one mile walk-in), fishing, climbing by permit only, snowmobiling, snowshoeing, cross-country skiing in forest and reservation.

Pets: Allowed on leash at falls area.

For more information:

Park Supervisor, Mount Washington State Forest, RFD 3, Mount Washington, MA 01258; 413-528-0330, or Region 5 Headquarters, Pittsfield State Forest, P.O. Box 1433, Pittsfield, MA 01202; 413-442-8928.

BARTHOLOMEW'S COBBLE

More than 700 species of plants are found at Bartholomew's Cobble, a delightful place for the serious botanist

Raccoons make themselves at home almost anywhere

and the casual nature lover alike. The plants thrive in the lime-rich soils of the 277-acre reservation in the tiny town of Ashley Falls.

The natural rock garden beside the Housatonic River is recognized by the National Park Service as a National Natural Landmark. The designation is justly deserved. So is the cobble's claim as home to the state's best display of ferns. Over forty-four ferns and related species grow here — maidenhair and marsh fern, ostrich and cinnamon fern, club mosses and horsetails.

The diverse plant life supports white-tailed deer, red fox, beavers, woodchucks, raccoons, cottontail rabbits, squirrels, and chipmunks. Birds flock to the cobble, either as a flyway during spring and fall migrations or as a place for nesting. Over 240 species have been recorded. I was entertained by a raucous kingfisher diving for fish in the Half River Elbow.

The reservation is named for George Bartholomew, who farmed the surrounding land in the 1880s.

All the beauty and life is due to the 500-year-old limestone outcrops called cobbles. The quartzite and marble forms soils dear to the alkaline-loving plants. The proximity of the Housatonic River enriches the area further.

The Trustees of Reservations maintains the cobble, and its six-mile Ledges Interpretive Trail loops through the woodlands. A booklet is available for the self-guided tour that introduces the visitor to the cobble's natural history and plant life. The West Fence Trail and Tulip Tree Trail climb to the top of Hurlburt's Hill for a sweeping view of the Housatonic Valley in the southern Berkshires.

The Bailey Trail and Spero Trail provide enjoyable walks through floodplain forest and meadows adjacent to the Housatonic River. Huge cottonwoods are found along the Bailey Trail.

A lucky visitor might see bank swallows ducking into holes in the riverbanks where their nests are. Butterflies are abundant, especially in the open fields. Flowering plants bloom through spring, summer, and fall. Each takes its turn: hepatica, violets, trillium, red columbine, Dutchman's-breeches, harebell, saxifrage, black-eyed Susans, and asters.

The Housatonic and Half Rivers offer the treats. Ducks and geese are usually seen. Even in winter they gather on ice-free sections.

Other times of the year painted turtles sun themselves on snags. I counted a dozen during one visit. My approach startled them and they slipped into the water. One by one they resurfaced and jockeyed for position on a fallen tree. But it was back into the water when a muskrat swam too close for their comfort.

Where: From Sheffield Center take State 7 south 1.6 miles. Turn right onto State 7A and follow for one-half mile. Turn right onto Rannapo Road and follow for 1.5 miles to Weatogue Road. Entrance is on left.
Hours: Trails open daily 9:00 A.M. to 5:00 P.M. year-round. The rustic Bailey Natural History Museum is open Wednesday through Sunday 9:00 A.M. to 5:00 P.M. mid-April to mid-October.
Admission: A nominal fee is charged.
Best time to visit: Spring through early fall.

Activities: Hiking, cross-country skiing, photography, plant, bird and wildlife observation, picnicking, canoeing.
Pets: Allowed on leash.
Other: The Colonel John Ashley House is located on the reservation. Built in 1835, it is one of the oldest houses in Berkshire County and is on the National Register of Historic Places. Guided tours are offered seasonally. 413-298-8600.
For more information:
   Trustees of Reservations, P.O. Box 792, Stockbridge, MA 01262; 413-298-3239.

MONUMENT MOUNTAIN RESERVATION

Light-colored quartzite rock and a steep eastern slope with a jumble of boulders gives Monument Mountain a distinctive look.

   The 1,640-foot Squaw Peak atop the mountain provides fine views west to the Taconic Range, east to the Hoosac Range, north to Mount Greylock, and south to Mount Everett. The scenery is outstanding during the height of the fall foliage.

   The Trustees of Reservations manages the 503-acre reservation in Great Barrington and maintains two trails to the summit. The 1.25-mile Indian Mountain Trail starts at the southern end of the parking lot. It is a gentle stretch. The three-quarter-mile Hickey Trail begins on the northern end of the parking lot. It is moderately steep and badly eroded in places. It passes a small waterfall and rock boulder which honors Rosalie Butler, who conveyed the land to Massachusetts in 1899. In early summer mountain laurel and sheep laurel in full bloom cover the woodland.

The two trails meet just below the summit for the short but rugged final ascent through low-bush blueberry, pine, and dwarfed northern red oak to the exposed top of Squaw Peak.

As you follow the trail along the precipitous edge, the cliffs seem to just fall away. It's no place for the faint-hearted. The top of the mountain is a series of quartzite rock outcrops. The most striking is a pile of white rock known as "Devil's Pulpit."

The summit is a good place to observe migrating birds, particularly a hawk flight in the spring. Hawks and turkey vultures fly over in lesser numbers in the autumn.

The most famous visitors to Monument Mountain were Nathaniel Hawthorne and Herman Melville. The writers supposedly met for the first time in August of 1850 and hiked to the top for a picnic.

Where: From Massachusetts Turnpike take exit 2 in Lee. Follow State 102 to Stockbridge. Follow State 7 south for five miles. Parking lot is on right.
Hours: Sunrise to sunset year-round. Donation requested.
Best time to visit: Spring, summer, fall.
Activities: Hiking, picnicking.
Pets: Allowed on leash.
For more information:
Trustees of Reservations, Western Regional Office, P.O. Box 792, Stockbridge, MA 01262; 413-298-3239.

ICE GLEN

Ice Glen is a half-mile gorge strewn with boulders and fallen hemlocks. A wave of cool air greets visitors.

Ice remains in the glen into early summer, lingering in deep crevices. Steam forms as the cold moisture rises. Even in midday the place is a bit eerie. In fact, the town of Stockbridge holds a torchlight parade through the glen on Halloween.

Huge hemlocks and white pine line the sides, letting in little sunlight and helping create the cool conditions.

A blue-blazed trail leads the way through the maze. It's a scramble over moss-covered rocks. It's quite slippery in spring when ice coats the boulders.

At the northern end of the ravine a trail leads to Laura's Tower. The twenty-five-foot-high metal tower rises just above the treetops of birch, American beech, maples, and oaks. I shared the platform with two couples from New York who enjoyed a picnic—complete with red-and-white checkered tablecloth.

Where: Take State 7 south from Stockbridge center and turn left onto Ice Glen Road. The trail, marked with a small sign, begins on the left on a private driveway. Park on the side of the road.
Hours: Sunrise to sunset.
Best time to visit: Summer and fall. Trails are accessible in winter and spring but are icy.
Activities: Hiking, picnicking.
Pets: Allowed.

For more information:
Laurel Hill Association maintains trails. Call Stockbridge Town Hall; 413-298-4714.

PITTSFIELD STATE FOREST

This is my idea of camping. My tent is pitched on the edge of Berry Pond, the highest natural body of water in Massachusetts at 2,150 feet.

Surprisingly for its size—9,695 acres—Pittsfield State Forest is often overlooked, standing as it does between two larger neighbors, Mount Greylock State Reservation and October State Forest. Anyone who ignores it is missing a gem.

Since the crowds go elsewhere, it's easy to secure a campsite most anytime, even on holiday weekends, and walk on the footpaths in near solitude.

Fishermen can cast a line from shore or boat and catch a trout in stream-fed Berry Pond. Then cook the succulent fish in the frying pan on the grill at your campsite.

The thirteen campsites on the pond's southern shore are not for the comfort-loving camper. The sites are primitive. Dig pit toilets and bring your own water. But it's cheap ($8) and the setting is worth the inconvenience. Campsites ($10) with running water and flush toilets are available below Berry Pond near forest headquarters.

Pittsfield State Forest is a haven for hikers. Thirty miles of trails crisscross the hillsides and woodlands, where maples, red oaks, and hawthorns grow. Mountain bikes and horses are welcome on designated trails.

Two interstate trails, Taconic Crest Trail and Taconic Skyline Trail, travel through the western edge, giving the ambitious hiker a chance for a more venturesome outing. Taconic Crest Trail travels north twenty-three miles from Berry Pond to Pownal, Vermont, while Skyline Trail runs twenty-three miles from Richmond north to Williamstown. It crosses over the surrounding Berkshire Hills and across into New York. The scenery is splendid in the fall when the trees are ablaze in colorful foliage.

On a more modest level, Berkshire Hills Ramble and Woods Ramble are one-mile, self-guided nature trails. Brochures for both are available at forest headquarters. The two trails combine lessons in nature with pleasant scenery. Berkshire Hills Ramble goes through a twenty-acre field of azaleas. Woods Ramble tells the story of a new forest born in the mid-1800s after the original forest was cut by settlers for firewood and used as pastureland.

One of the new wheelchair-accessible trails in the Massachusetts parks and forest system is found at Pittsfield State Forest. The asphalt-paved Tranquility Trail makes a half-mile loop through the woods. A wheelchair-accessible restroom and picnic area are nearby.

Lulu Pond lures the hiker for a refreshing swim.

The forest is just as much fun to visit in winter. There's a well-marked trail system for cross-country skiers and another for snowmobiles. A rustic lodge built in the 1930s by the Civilian Conservation Corps is available for group rental.

Where: Take Massachusetts Turnpike west to exit 2 in

Lee. Follow State 7 north to downtown Pittsfield. Turn left onto West Street. Go past Onota Lake and take a right on Churchill Street and a left onto Cascade Street. Entrance is at end of road.

Hours: Sunrise to sunset.

Best time to visit: Year-round.

Activities: Hiking, camping, picnicking, swimming, fishing, cross-country skiing, snowmobiling, snowshoeing.

Pets: Allowed on leash.

Other: October State Forest is back in Lee. At 16,000 acres it is the largest state forest in Massachusetts. It's extremely popular with hunters and snowmobilers.

The most scenic trail goes through the 1.5-mile Schermerhorn Gorge. Fifty campsites are available; some are wheelchair accessible.

For more information:

Pittsfield State Forest, Cascade Street, Pittsfield, MA 01201; 413-442-8892. October State Forest, Woodland Road, Lee, MA 01238; 413-243-1778.

MOUNT GREYLOCK STATE RESERVATION

Fog enshrouded the summit of Mount Greylock, and a strong, cold wind blew as I began my descent down the Hopper Trail past balsam fir, whose growth is stunted by harsh conditions.

Mount Greylock is close to being a wilderness. The 3,491-foot peak is the state's highest. Its upper 900 feet resemble a boreal community, a northern forest found most often in New Hampshire's White Mountains and Canada.

Red Spruce and yellow birch grow on the cool, wet northern reaches. The only northern mountain ash in Massachusetts is found on Mount Greylock. Sphagnum moss thrives in isolated bogs.

On a clear day the summit offers views of up to 100 miles across Massachusetts and into New York, Vermont, and New Hampshire. The ninety-two-foot War Veterans Memorial Tower atop the rocky peak is open daily during summer and fall. Weather conditions can change rapidly. Thirty minutes before fog enveloped the area, dawn's sunlight had streaked the sky.

I had stayed overnight at venerable Bascom Lodge, which provides accommodations for thirty-two people from mid-May through mid-October. The two-story rustic stone and wood lodge offers both dormitory-style rooms and private ones, and meals served family style.

A favorite pastime of overnight guests is to gather around the stone fireplace in the great room after dinner and share stories about hiking and other outdoor experiences. On this evening someone brought up five black bear sightings reported in early September.

I had spent the previous night at Sperry Campground located about 2.5 miles below the summit. The Massachusetts Division of Forest and Parks maintains the camping area of thirty-five individual and five group sites. It provides easy access to several trails, including footpaths to Deer Hill Falls and spectacular March Cataract.

The 12,500-acre reservation contains forty-five miles of trails. Nearly eight miles of the famed Appalachian Trail dissect the reservation on its 2,155-mile journey from Georgia to Maine. Appalachian Trail users often sign registers at Bascom Lodge and elsewhere along the route. The weather-beaten blue notebook at the trail intersection on Mount Williams was full of inscriptions, both serious and humorous, describing trail conditions, the weather and hikers' state of mind.

First-time visitors should stop at the visitors center at the Rockwell Road entrance on the southern side of the reservation. The center contains exhibits about the reservation's geology, birds, and other wildlife. Trail maps are available, and staff from the Division of Forests and Parks and the Appalachian Mountain Club are on hand to answer questions. Rockwell Road and Notch Road go to the summit and are open mid-May to early November, weather permitting.

Debate continues on whether the name Greylock refers to the gray clouds and mists that often surround the peak, or Chief Gray-lock, a leader of the Waranock Indians who once lived in the region.

With so large an area it's best to tackle one section at a time. The Hopper is a good place to start. The bowl-shaped valley contains old-growth forest with stands of red spruce more than 200 years old. The National Park Service has designated the area a National Natural Landmark.

The most spectacular view of the Hopper is from Stony Ledge, which is easily reached via Sperry Road. A more strenuous route, open to hikers and mountain bike riders, is Stony Ledge Trail. It starts far below at Goodell Hollow.

The rock outcropping known as Stony Ledge drops 1,400 feet. It affords a sweeping view that encompasses the west slope of Mount Greylock, Mount Fitch (3,100 feet), Mount Williams (2,951), and Mount Prospect (2,690). Hopper and Money Brooks ramble through the valley below and March Cataract roars in the distance. The common raven and other birds add their voices to the sounds of nature.

Hopper Trail begins on farmland off the dirt Hopper Road. It shares the path with Money Brook Trail for a short distance through pastureland before Money Brook swings left and Hopper heads right and begins a steady, moderately strenuous climb. The blue-blazed trail goes through a forest of northern hardwood and basswood. In springtime, hepatica, Dutchman's-breeches, and other flowers color the forest floor. But autumn is my favorite time. The deep green of conifers provides a background for brilliant red, yellow, and orange foliage of maple, beech, birch, and oak.

In about an hour, the trail reaches Sperry Road Campground. The trail follows the road for a short distance, and then reenters the woods on the left, where it continues the ascent to the summit, which takes another half-hour to reach.

A 6.5-mile loop is possible by taking the Appalachian Trail north from the summit to Mount Fitch and then down Money Brook Trail. A side path leads to Money Brook Falls, tucked deep into the hillside. One can swing even farther north on the Appalachian Trail and climb over Mount Williams, go across Mount Prospect Trail, and then join Money Brook Trail. The descent from Mount Prospect to Money Brook is one of the steepest and roughest in the reservation.

Two good choices for side trips are Overlook Trail, which features three scenic outlooks across the Hopper, and March Cataract Trail, which leads to the tallest and most spectacular waterfall in the reservation. The flow of water at March Cataract and other waterfalls is highest in the spring. I find them most beautiful when they are coated in layers of ice in late fall or early spring. For the expert and well-prepared outdoor enthusiast, they are worth the trek in the winter.

One of the most popular routes to the summit is up the southern slope via the Appalachian Trail. A parking lot off Rockwell Road provides access to the trail, which climbs up Jones Nose, a promontory with fine views to the southeast. The AT follows the ridge line over Saddle Ball Mountain. Birches and oak dominate the forest. Jones Nose is one of the few open areas in the reservation. Blueberry bushes, chokeberry, and mountain ash grow here. Flowers are bountiful in the sun-drenched meadows.

A variety of birds are found around the reservation. Thrushes are plentiful: there are veery, gray-cheeked, wood, and Swainson's. The tapping of pileated woodpeckers is sometimes heard as well as the singing of white-throated sparrows, junco, and warblers. It's not uncommon to startle grouse while one walks along the trails. Turkey vultures and red-tailed hawks fly overhead in strong wind currents.

Small animals such as red and gray squirrels, woodchucks, raccoons, porcupines, and snowshoe hare inhabit the reservation. So do coyote, fisher, white-tailed deer, black bear, and bobcat.

Rockwell Road and Notch Road become main routes for snowmobilers and cross-country skiers. Either road is an arduous eight-mile trek to the summit for the skier. Howling winds and bitter cold often await. So do spectacular views on clear, crisp days. And so does a hair-raising descent.

Expert backcountry skiers tackle the Thunderbolt Trail, Bellows Pipe Trail (both expert ski trails carved out in the 1930s), Stony Ledge Trail, CCC Dynamite Trail, and a section of the Hopper Trail. These trails and other hiking trails used by snowshoers cut through the forest's deep snows and ice-coated rocks and trees. Seeing what plant and animal life must endure during a grueling winter increases one's appreciation of their ability to survive.

Where: Take State 2 west to North Adams. To enter from the north turn left one mile from downtown onto Notch Road. Follow to entrance gate. Another choice is to take the Massachusetts Turnpike west to exit 2 in Lee. Go north to Pittsfield. Follow State 7/20 north. Turn right onto Rockwell Road. Reach visitors center in one mile.

Hours: Open sunrise to half-hour after sunset. The visitors center is open 9:00 A.M. to 5:00 P.M. daily mid-May to mid-October, and 8:00 A.M. to 4:00 P.M. weekends and holidays mid-October to May. Notch Road and Rockwell Road to the summit are open mid-May to early November, weather permitting. War Veterans Memorial Tower is open 9:00 A.M. to 5:00 P.M. mid-May to mid-October.

Best time to visit: Year-round. Fall foliage is spectacular. Winter access is limited to snowmobilers and by foot.

Activities: Hiking, mountain bike riding, picnicking, camping, hunting (in season), snowmobiling, snowshoeing, cross-country skiing, interpretive programs.

Pets: Allowed on leash.

Other: Bascom Lodge is open mid-May to mid-October. Cost for bunk bed is $30 (adult) and $19 (child). Private room is $70. Dinner is $10, breakfast is $5 and trail lodge is $5. Reservations are recommended.

Speery Campground provides thirty-five individual and group sites. There are fireplaces and running water, but no showers or flush toilets. Sites are first-come first-served. Groups of five or more need reservations. Cost is $8 for individual site, $16 for group site.

Lean-to shelters are located off the Appalachian Trail in Wilbur's Crossing and near Peck's Falls off the Gould Trail.

For more information:

Mount Greylock State Reservation, Rockwell Road, Lanesborough, MA 01237; 413-499-4262 or 413-499-4263. Bascom Lodge: 413-743-1591. Appalachian Mountain Club: 413-443-0011.

NATURAL BRIDGE STATE PARK

Natural Bridge State Park contains the only marble bridge in North America carved out by water. The bridge was formed about 13,000 years ago during the retreat of the last glacier that covered New England. Meltwaters sculpted the Hudson Brook Chasm and the bridge. Hundreds of millions of years earlier, heat and pressure during the mountain formation process had transformed limestone into marble.

Hudson Brook, a tributary of the Hoosic River, continues to slowly wear away the chasm walls below Natural Bridge. Water volume is highest in the spring when rain and snowmelt turn the brook into a powerful torrent.

Walkways on the chasm sides lead visitors down sixty feet for a close observation of the water rumbling through the 475-foot-long gorge. In summer, when the water is lower, algae, lichen, and mosses cling to the sides of the steep walls. Ferns that favor limestone also grow in the chasm.

The Natural Bridge spanning the chasm is twenty feet long and fifteen feet wide. Just upstream from the bridge is the only white marble dam in North America.

A park ranger is on duty to answer questions. Signs with brief explanations on how nature created the unusual formation are found along the walkway.

Platforms from which to view the chasm are located along the fenced, wooden walkways. The view east from the top of the chasm looks toward the West Summit on the Mohawk Trail.

An abandoned marble quarry is adjacent to the bridge. The quarry produced coarse-grained white marble in the 1880s.

The Massachusetts Department of Environmental Management oversees the forty-nine-acre park.

Where: From downtown North Adams follow State 8 (Beaver Street) north one-half mile. Turn left on McCauley Road to park entrance and parking lot above the old quarry.

Hours: Open daily 10:00 A.M. to 6:00 P.M. Memorial Day to late October.

Admission: Small fee.

Pets: Allowed on leash.

Activities: Observing natural historic site, picnicking.

Other: Clarksburg State Park and Clarksburg State Forest are nearby. Directions to state park: from State 8 north, take Middle Road in Clarksburg; to state forest: take State 2 to Blackington to West Road north.

The state park contains a day-use area offering swimming, picnicking, and fishing. A scenic trail encircles Mauserts Pond. Fifty campsites are located near the lake.

The Appalachian Trail passes through the 2,933-acre state forest. The area is popular with hunters, hikers, cross-country skiers, and snowmobilers.

For more information:

Natural Bridge State Park, Route 8, North Adams, MA 01247; 413-663-6392 in summer; 413-663-6312 in winter.

Clarksburg State Park and Clarksburg State Forest, Middle Road, Clarksburg, MA; 413-664-8345 in summer; 413-442-8928 in winter.

WINDSOR JAMBS STATE PARK/
WINDSOR STATE FOREST

When you're standing at the top of the Windsor Jambs,

the roar is deafening as the water eighty feet below surges headlong through the chasm.

Swollen with snowmelt and early spring rains, Windsor Jambs Brook, a tributary of the Westfield River, is wild and frothy. It bounces off sheer walls of the twenty-five-foot-wide gorge. It scurries over boulders, fallen trees, and blocks of ice. Nothing blocks its path through the quarter-mile-long gorge.

Windsor Jambs is the jewel of the 1,626-acre Windsor State Forest in the Berkshire foothills. The gorge cuts through thick groves of red spruce and eastern hemlock. A footpath, with a metal safety fence, runs along the top of the gorge's western side.

The forest is home year-round to red squirrels, who seem to chatter incessantly. White-tailed deer fancy the place as well. There was an old set of black bear tracks across the footpath the day I took to the Jambs.

There are two approaches to the ravine. You can walk the three-mile Jambs Trail that starts at the campground near the forest headquarters, or you can drive up the gravel Lower Road to a parking lot at the top of the gorge.

Where: Take State 9 west from Northampton twenty-two miles to Windsor. Turn right at the Windsor Jambs–West Cummington road sign and go one mile through West Cummington. Turn right onto River Road and follow west three miles to Windsor State Forest.

Hours: Year-round. Parking areas close at 8:00 P.M.

Activities: Hiking, picnicking, swimming, camping, fishing, hunting in season, cross-country skiing, snowshoeing, snowmobiling.

Pets: Allowed on leash.

Other: The three-mile Steep Bank Brook Trail connects Windsor State Forest to Notchview State Reservation. The Trustees of Reservations maintains the 3,000-acre reservation, which contains twenty-five miles of trails open to hikers and cross-country skiers. It can be reached by car off State 9, about five miles west of the turnoff for Windsor State Forest.

For more information:

Windsor State Forest, River Road, Windsor, MA 01270; 413-684-0984. Notchview State Reservation: 413-684-0148.

CHESTERFIELD GORGE

The West Branch of the Westfield River rushes through Chesterfield Gorge before it flattens out 1,000 feet down river.

The water is most forceful and wild in the spring when it races over boulders and snags. The volume of water – and noise – is turned up to the max.

Trustees of Reservations is caretaker of the gorge and of the 161-acre reservation in West Cummington.

A footpath to the left of a red wooden building beside the parking lot leads to the river's edge. Upstream the river sweeps around the bend and rambles over the first in a series of cascades. Pools at the bottom of each cascade are deep and clear.

Remnants of High Bridge are visible on both sides of the gorge's entrance. The bridge was built in 1739 and spanned the gorge as part of the Boston to Albany Post Road.

Another foot trail with a metal safety fence runs along the top of the gorge. It offers views down into the ravine. Tall and stately hemlock, ash, and oak grow on both sides of the chasm.

Where: Take State 9 west from Northampton nine miles to Williamsburg and turn left onto State 143. Follow west ten miles to West Chesterfield. Cross the West Chesterfield Bridge and take the first left onto Ireland Street. Follow west .8 mile to River Road. Entrance and parking are on left.
Hours: Open daily 8:00 A.M. to sunset May 1 to October 30. A small fee is charged.
Best time to visit: Water level is highest in spring.
Activities: Walking, picnicking, trout fishing.
Pets: Allowed on leash.
For more information:
Trustees of Reservations, Western Regional Office, The Mission House, P.O. Box 792, Stockbridge, MA 01262; 413-298-3229 or 413-684-0184.

BRIDGE OF FLOWERS/GLACIAL POTHOLES

The Bridge of Flowers graces the Deerfield River in Shelburne Falls on the scenic Mohawk Trail.

Colorful flowers, vines, and shrubs adorn the former trolley bridge. Canterbury bells, bachelor buttons, petunias, and roses were among the hundreds of flowers in bloom during my visit on a delightful sun-splashed day in June. Butterflies danced from flower to flower.

Over 500 species of plants are found on the bridge.

With so much diversity, flowers are in bloom from spring through fall. Vines hang over the sides of the five arches.

Members of the Shelburne Falls Women's Club volunteer their time to meticulously maintain the rows of flower beds. Their tender loving care is obvious.

Today's flowers grow where trolleys once traveled. The bridge was built in 1908 to carry trolleys over the river. It did so for twenty years until it was abandoned in 1928. Its demise was short-lived. The following year, at the urging of Walter and Antoinette Burnham, money was raised to turn the bridge into a pathway of plants. Today the unique bridge is acclaimed internationally.

Just down the river from the Bridge of Flowers lies the Glacial Potholes, a cluster of circular holes in the Deerfield River bed. Stairs lead down to the river's edge. Looking back upstream one sees a layered array of colorful rocks. Large pools lie at the foot of the cascading water.

The potholes were created by the grinding action of the gravel trapped in the bedrock cracks and whirled around by the water. Some are six inches in diameter. Others are several feet wide.

Richard D. Little, a geology professor at Greenfield Community College, is an authority on the potholes. According to his book, *Exploring Franklin County, A Geology Guide,* light colors in the rocks are former sand grains metamorphosed into quartz and feldspar. Dark colors are former ash deposits of old volcanos transformed into the mineral hornblende. The orange is actually rust. Even if you're not a geology buff, the potholes are worth a visit just for their unusual look.

Where: Take I-91 to exit 26 in Greenfield. Follow State 2 west for nine miles. Turn left onto South Maple Street at sign for Shelburne Falls. Veer left onto Bridge Street. Signs lead to bridge and potholes.
Hours: Sunrise to sunset.
Best time to visit: Spring, summer, fall.
Admission: Free.
Activities: Walking, flower and geology study.
Pets: No.
Other: State 2 is the famous Mohawk Trail. It runs along the Deerfield River in stretches. There are places for picnicking, hiking, camping, whitewater rafting, hot-air ballooning, maple sugar sampling, and sightseeing from summit observation towers.
For more information:
    Franklin County Chamber of Commerce; 413-773-5463.

NORTHFIELD MOUNTAIN
CONNECTICUT RIVER BOAT RIDE

The wooden-hulled *Quinnetukut II* gently left its mooring and glided south across the smooth waters of the Connecticut River. It was a cool mid-October morning, made even cooler by the breeze the boat created.

Attention was drawn to the river's banks, which rise sharply on the left and on the right and become nearly vertical cliffs. Oaks, maples, and birches on the slopes of French King Gorge were ablaze in their fall foliage finery of red, orange, and yellow.

Quinnetukut II slipped past French King Rock and

under French King Bridge before it rounded a bend and headed west toward Barton Cove.

The 1.5-hour excursion is a learning experience. The two-member crew points out wildlife and provides commentary on geological features and the river's uses.

Native Americans named the river Quinnetukut, or "Long Tidal River." When it passes through Northfield, the river has traveled 286 miles from the Connecticut Lakes on the New Hampshire–Canada border and has another 123 miles to go to Long Island Sound.

French King Gorge is a narrows formed millions of years ago. Sedimentary rocks on the right and older, harder metamorphic rocks on the left have undergone years of erosion and glacial activity.

As *Quinnetuket II* approaches Barton Cove, passengers search treetops for American bald eagles. Soon the distinctive white head and tail of a mature one are spotted. It sits elegantly on the top branch of a bare tree. Another tree holds a nest. We are told that eagles build nests of sticks and pine boughs thirty to 120 feet off the ground in hardwood or conifer trees. Some nests are eight feet wide.

The eagle at Barton Cove is believed to be one of the forty-one birds released from 1981 to 1988 at Quabbin Reservoir east of Northfield.

After allowing passengers a final look at the magnificent birds, the boat's captain turns *Quinnetukut II* upriver for the six-mile return.

Northfield Mountain Recreation and Environmental Center offers the river excursions. Northeast Utilities operates the center, which contains twenty-five miles of trails for hiking, cross-country skiing, snowshoeing, and mountain bike riding, plus offering an orienteering course and fitness trail.

Where: Take State 2 to State 63 north. Northfield is on the right.
Hours: Open 9:00 A.M. to 5:00 P.M. Wednesday through Sunday, April through November, and daily during winter for cross-country skiing. Riverboat season runs from late May to mid-October, weather permitting. Reservations required. Cost is $7 for adults, $6 for seniors fifty-five and older, $3 for children.
Best time to visit: Year-round.
Admission: Trail use is free except for cross-country skiing.
Pets: No.
Activities: Hiking, picnicking, cross-country skiing, snowshoeing, mountain bike riding, boat rides, horseback riding, orienteering, fitness trail, geology study, bird observation.
Other: Bus tours are available spring through fall to the 300-acre reservoir atop Northfield Mountain and the hydroelectric power generating facility. Interpretive programs are available at Barton Cove from mid-May to Labor Day.
For more information:
    Northfield Mountain Recreation and Environmental Center, RR 2, Box 117, Northfield, MA 01360; 413-659-3714.

CONNECTICUT RIVER FISHWAYS

Every spring they arrive, first just a few, then by the hundreds, and finally by the thousands. It's the American shad's annual spawning migration up the Connecticut River.

For an up-close look at the ritual, visit Northeast

In mid-April shad begin to migrate up the Connecticut River

Utilities' fishways at Holyoke Dam and Turner's Falls Dam. Viewing areas open in early May. Water level and temperature dictate the progress of the fish upstream, so the opening date varies each year.

My visit to the Holyoke Dam occurred on a day when thousands of shad hitched a ride up and over the dam. It looked like a rush as they passed the glass windows in the viewing area, swimming through a 300-foot-long flume. They had just gotten an elevator ride fifty-two feet up from the tailrace. In some years over 500,000 shad are lifted over the dam.

Snakelike eels swam past as well. But to my disappointment, I didn't see an Atlantic salmon. A major effort to restore Atlantic salmon to the Connecticut was started in the 1980s. After the program's initial success, salmon returns have slowed.

American shad and Atlantic salmon are anadromous fish. As such, they are born in fresh water, mature in the ocean, and return to the rivers where they were born to spawn. American shad migrate in spring; Atlantic salmon mostly migrate in spring, although some do so in fall.

For American shad, the journey begins in mid-April when they leave Long Island Sound and head north up the 410-mile Connecticut River. These adult fish lived four to six years at sea.

As early as 1955 the Holyoke Water Power Company began a rudimentary fish ladder, employing an elevator, hand nets, and barrels. A far more efficient system has since evolved. In Holyoke, an elevator lifts fish over the dam. In Turner's Falls, the fish swim up a series of ladders.

Further upriver are fishways at Vernon, Bellows Falls, and Wilder dams, opening the river for migration from Connecticut to New Hampshire.

Where: Take I-91 to exit 16 in Holyoke and take State 116 north. Holyoke Fishway is located off Bridge Street (State 11), just west of the Old County Bridge. For Turner's Falls Fishway take I-91 to exit 27 in Greenfield. Follow State 2 east to Turner's Falls. Viewing facility is on First Street, off Avenue A.
Hours: Wednesday through Sunday, 9:00 A.M. to 5:00 P.M., early May to mid-June.
Admission: Free.
Activities: Fish viewing. Guides provide information about the natural history of anadromous fish and the restoration program of the Connecticut River.
For more information:
Northfield Mountain Recreation and Environmental Center, RR 2, Box 117, Northfield, MA 01360; 413-659-3714. Holyoke Water Power Company, 1 Canal Street, Holyoke, MA 01040; 413-536-5520.

HOLYOKE RANGE STATE PARK/
SKINNER STATE PARK

Take your pick. On the western end of the Holyoke Range is Mount Holyoke (878 feet) with scenic vistas of the Connecticut River Valley. On the eastern end seven miles away stands Mount Norowottuck (1,106 feet) with its 250-foot eastern cliff.

In between lies a series of hills separated by sharp, deep valleys. Holyoke Range State Park consists of nearly 3,000 acres and encompasses Skinner State Park. The range is unusual in that it runs west to east rather than south to north. The unusual alignment creates two distinct forest habitats, with the ridge line forming the boundary between the two. On the southern slope oaks and hickories grow in an environment that is dryer and warmer than on the north side, which is steep, cool, and moist and supports hemlocks, white pines, beeches, and birches.

The notch splits the range into two sections. State 116 passes through it and provides access to the Notch Visitor Center, a good place to begin your exploration and obtain a trail map.

There are forty-five miles of trails, including eleven miles of the Metacomet-Monadnock Trail. I followed it east from the Notch Visitor Center two miles to Mount Norwottuck. Hidden 150 feet below the summit are weathered rocks and ledges known as the Horse Caves. It was here that Daniel Shays and his followers hid their horses during Shays Rebellion. Today, a narrow path scrambles around rock shelters. Moss and lichens cover the ledges.

Mount Holyoke is five miles west of the Notch Visitors Center. I took the M & M Trail, a strenuous hike over Bare Mountain (1,010 feet), Mt. Hitchcock (1,005), the Seven Sisters, and Taylor's Notch.

Mount Holyoke is the site of the historic Summit House, which has been restored to its appearance of the 1880s. The one-room structure was one of the earliest mountain-top inns in North America when it opened in 1821. There still are remains of the steam-powered tram that took visitors from the halfway area to the summit.

Mount Holyoke affords spectacular views of the valley lowlands and the Connecticut River. Mount Tom Range lies to the south.

An easier way to the summit is the auto road that begins at the entrance of Mountain Road. Trails to the summit begin here as well.

Where: Take I-91 to exit 19 in Northampton. Follow State 9 west to State 47 south. Turn left onto Mountain Road and entrance to Skinner State Park. To reach Notch Visitors Center continue on State 9 west to Amherst center and turn right onto State 116. Follow south. Entrance is on left.

Hours: Mount Holyoke summit road is open mid-April to mid-November. The summit house is open mid-May to mid-October. Notch Visitors Center is open year-round, 9:00 A.M. to 4:00 P.M. daily. Closed Tuesday and Wednesday in winter.

Activities: Hiking, picnicking, horseback riding, interpretive programs, cross-country skiing, snowshoeing.

Pets: Allowed on leash.

For more information:

Holyoke Range State Park, 1500 West Street, Amherst, MA 01002; 413-253-2883. Skinner State Park, Box 91, Route 47, Hadley, MA 01035; 413-586-0350 or 413-253-2883.

QUABBIN RESERVOIR PARK AND RESERVATION

Enfield Lookout, one of the best and most accessible places from which to look at eagles at Quabbin Reservoir, did not disappoint.

Five of the magnificent birds were sighted during one of my visits on a cold, blustery day in early January. All were mature eagles, at least five or six years old. Only the adult bald eagle has the distinctive white tail and head. Its wingspan extends seven feet.

Go to Enfield Lookout to spot eagles

Immature bald eagles generally are completely brown, although some may have a few white feathers.

It takes practice to spot an eagle in the vast terrain. High-powered binoculars or a scope is a must. A group of dedicated eagle watchers set up their equipment practically every Saturday and Sunday during the winter when the eagles come to the area for the abundant food supply. Some of the birds are part of an eagle restoration program begun at Quabbin a decade ago.

Enfield Lookout is a high promontory on the southern end of the reservoir, which covers thirty-nine square miles and is the largest in Massachusetts. It looks out across to Prescott Peninsula, where eagles are most often seen.

It takes a trained eye to pick out an eagle a mile away. The white head is distinctive, but it also blends into a backdrop of white snow. But luck was on our side. One eagle, then another, was spotted in the hemlock trees about twenty feet apart. It was the beginning of a wonderful afternoon. Later, an eagle was perched atop a barren tree when another swept down, drove the occupant off, and claimed the seat for its own. Even more spectacular was the flight of a bald eagle circling over the water, riding the updrafts. More than ten minutes passed before the eagle flew out of sight.

When winter's grip is strongest and the reservoir is frozen, a life-and-death struggle often takes place on the ice surface. Coyotes and packs of dogs chase down hungry and weak deer. The carcasses provide a source of food for eagles and other animals.

The scenes are reminders that Quabbin is essentially

a wilderness. It sprawls over 126 square miles. The reservoir has a shoreline of 118 miles and a 412-billion-gallon water capacity.

Four towns — Dana, Enfield, Prescott, and Greenwich — were flooded to create the reservoir in the Swift River Valley. Water covers remnants of the towns, where 2,500 people once lived. Construction of the reservoir began in 1926. The Windsor Dam and Goodnough Dam were finished in 1939, and it took another seven years for the reservoir to fill.

A visitors center in Quabbin Park in the southern end of the watershed in Belchertown contains exhibits on the transformation. Quabbin Park also contains eighteen miles of marked trails, old roadways and paved roads for hiking, designated picnic areas, and Quabbin Summit with a stone lookout tower.

The northern reaches in Petersham and Salem are more remote. Large areas of the reservation lands are closed to the public to protect watershed.

"The Big Lady," as the Quabbin is affectionately known, contains practically every kind of freshwater fish found in Massachusetts: lake, brown, and rainbow trout, landlocked salmon, bass, white and yellow perch, pickerel, and bullheads. The Quabbin fishing season opens the third Saturday in April.

Where: From Massachusetts Turnpike take exit 7. Follow State 21 northeast and then State 202 east fourteen miles to Belchertown Center. Take State 9 east for two miles. Entrance is on left.
Hours: Sunrise to sunset. Visitors center is open week-

EAGLE WATCHING

Quabbin Reservoir is a premier eagle-watching area. Here are a few hints for sightings. High-powered binoculars or viewing scope is a must.

Bald eagle: the most common variety found at Quabbin. The adult's head and tail are all white, and its beak is yellow. Wingspan may exceed seven feet. Wings are practically horizontal when it soars.

The immature bald eagle lacks the white head and tail. It is generally brown, but it may have a few white feathers. The bill is dark. Plumage turns gray as the bird matures. It gains white plumage at age five or six.

Golden eagle: only occasionally seen at Quabbin. Its bill is smaller than the bald eagle's and wings are broader. Plumage is dark, reddish brown.

The immature golden eagle is darker brown with white in the tail.

---

days, 8:30 A.M. to 5:00 P.M.; weekends 9:00 A.M. to 5:00 P.M. The main road is open year-round.

Best time to visit: Year-round. Winter is prime season for eagle watching.

Activities: Hiking, birdwatching, picnicking, snowshoeing. Cross-country skiing and snowmobiles are prohibited.

Pets: No.

For more information:

Metropolitan District Commission, Quabbin Park Visitors Center, 485 Ware Road, Belchertown, MA 01070; 413-323-7221.

2

Central
Massachusetts

HARVARD FOREST

The importance of bumpy ground in a forest, the role of
sprouting, the effects of lightning, the devastation of a
hurricane. All are explained – and examples of each are
found – in Harvard Forest in Petersham. The 3,000 acres
are living research laboratories in forest biology and
forestry.

Start your visit at Fisher Museum, which contains
twenty-three dioramas portraying the history of central
New England forests and exhibits on tree structures
and diseases. A collection of black-and-white photographs show the destruction wreaked by the Hurricane of
1938. One of the forest's tracts contains a demonstration

pulldown to simulate hurricane damage. Scientists monitor the site and collect data for the recovery of other areas where hurricanes strike.

The self-guided Natural History Trail and Black Gum Trail highlight interesting features of the forest: seeding beds; shady wood plants such as Indian cucumber root, New York fern, and wintergreen; the rebirth of woodland destroyed by fire; a swamp containing black gum trees. These trees, with egg-shaped leaves and round dark fruit, are rare in central New England. These are a treasure—some are more than 300 years old.

A pleasant hike is the 4.5-mile trail to Prospect Hill, where you can climb the fire tower for views of Wachusett Mountain, Mount Grace, and Mount Monadnock in southern New Hampshire.

Where: Harvard Forest is seventy miles west of Boston off State 2. At the junction of State 2 and State 32, take State 32 south three miles. Entrance to Fisher Museum is on left. From Worcester it is twenty-five miles northwest on State 122 and then 3.5 miles north from Petersham Center to State 32.

Hours: Fisher Museum is open 9:00 A.M. to 5:00 P.M. Monday through Friday year-round and 10:00 A.M. to 4:00 P.M. Saturday, May through October.

Best time to visit: Year-round.

Pets: Allowed on leash.

Activities: Walking, educational exhibits.

For more information:

Harvard Forest, Petersham, MA 01366; 508-724-3302.

DOANE'S FALLS

Doane's Falls in Royalston is a name seldom brought up when the state's most dramatic waterfalls are mentioned. What an oversight.

It's a gem. The waters of Lawrence Brook tumble down a series of five cascades, dropping 200 feet before they flatten out and join Tully River. Two cascades are twenty feet wide and plummet twenty feet to clear, deep pools.

The Trustees of Reservations oversees Doane's Falls and 31.5 acres that surround it.

A foot trail leads down one side of the brook and offers views of the falls from rock outcrops. Hemlock and pine stand atop the gorge's steep ledges. The trail is moderately steep in places. It ends at the foot of the last cascade, but a well-worn path continues to Tully Lake.

Where: From Boston take State 2 west to State 2A and State 32 in Athol; from Greenfield take State 2 east. In Athol, cross the Miller River bridge and turn right onto the Royalston-Athol Road. Follow four miles. Entrance is on left immediately after stone bridge over Lawrence Brook at Doane Hill Road.
Hours: Sunrise to sunset.
Pets: Allowed on leash.
Activities: Hiking, picnicking.
Other: Tully Lake Recreation Area in nearby Baldwinville offers twenty-one campsites, boat ramp, fishing, hunting in restricted areas, and snowmobiling. To reach the area take Doane Hill Road west and turn left onto Winchendon Road. Entrance is on left.

For more information:
Doane's Falls, Trustees of Reservations, Central Regional Office, Doyle Reservation, 325 Lindell Avenue, Leominster, MA 01453. 508-840-4464. Tully Lake Recreation Area, 508-939-8962

OTTER RIVER STATE FOREST/ LAKE DENNISON RECREATION AREA

I knew little about Otter River State Forest or Lake Dennison Recreation Area before my visit in mid-July. Dennison's size—9,000 acres—and lake (the forecast called for temperatures in the 90s) enticed me for a weekend camping trip.

The two adjacent areas are in the small towns of Baldwinville and Winchendon. The 4,200-acre Birch Hill Wildlife Management Area encompasses both.

I was lucky enough to secure a tent site near the lake shoreline. Dennison's two campgrounds contain 150 sites situated in stands of tall pines. Hot showers, trailer camp sites, and a trailer dumping station are available. Otter State Forest provides another 100 tent sites.

Lake Dennison is the focal point of activity. The day-use area contains a boat ramp and picnic and beach facilities. Even on a hot, midsummer day the lake was uncrowded, evidence that the area is a little-known haven.

The Wilder-McKenzie Nature Trail connects Dennison and the 1,200-acre Otter Forest. It takes roughly an hour to complete a circuit around the blue-blazed trail. The footpath winds through deep woodlands and reaches Beamon Pond. A side path goes to the Otter River State Forest campground.

Where: Take State 2 west to exit 20. Go right onto Baldwinville Road. Follow to State 202 north. Follow signs to entrance on left to Otter River State Forest. Lake Dennison entrance is two miles north on left.
Hours: Day-use (10:00 A.M. to sunset) and camping areas are open May to mid-October.
Admission: $2 for day use; $6 and $7 for camping.
Activities: Hiking, swimming, picnicking, canoeing, fishing, hunting in season, cross-country skiing, snowshoeing, snowmobiling, interpretive programs, walking.
Pets: Prohibited.
For more information:
   Otter River State Forest and Lake Dennison Recreation Area, State 202, Winchendon, MA 01436; 508-939-8962.

WACHUSETT MOUNTAIN STATE RESERVATION

Wachusett Mountain stands impressively at 2,006 feet, the highest point in Massachusetts east of the Berkshires.
   But the mountain is now a mere shadow of its original. It stood 23,000 feet high millions of years ago, but wind, water, and glacial erosion wore it down. Now it is a monadnock, an isolated mountain towering over the relatively flat surrounding terrain.
   The open summit offers panoramic views in every

direction. The most stunning are north to New Hampshire's Mount Monadnock and east to the Boston skyline. They were impressive even as I tried to hold my ground against a bracing wind on a late November day. It was cold at the top. A thin layer of ice coated some rocks. Snow-making guns were in action at Wachusett Mountain's downhill ski area on the western slope.

I pulled up my collar and enjoyed the views, a reward for my thirty-minute hike from the visitors center up Bicentennial Trail and Deer Hill Trail. It seemed appropriate that I descended Jack Frost Trail.

The hiker can traverse the reservation's 2,000 acres over approximately twenty miles of trails, including nearly four miles of the Midstate Trail. This long-distance footpath travels the length of Worcester County, eighty-five miles from Douglas State Forest on the Rhode Island border to Ashburnham near the New Hampshire line. It passes over Wachusett's summit along the way.

An auto road offers another way to reach the summit from mid-April through October 31.

In winter cross-country skiers and snowmobilers take over the roads and trails. On a return visit in February, I found out that the auto road provides an exhilarating descent on cross-country skis. I toiled and plodded up to the summit, but I had to dig in my ski edges and hang on for dear life on the way down.

Wachusett Mountain's history is steeped in Indian lore. Trail names—Old Indian and Sumuhanna—are reminders of the past. In fact, Wachusett means "by the Great Hill" in Algonquian.

Hemlock, pine, maple, spruce, beech, and birch

trees cover the reservation. An old-growth stand of northern red oak is found on the reservation's northern edge. Among wildflowers are trailing arbutus, mountain laurel, mayflower, and asters.

Where: From Boston take State 2 west to exit 25 for Westminster-Princeton. Take State 140 south to Mountain Road. From Massachusetts Turnpike take exit 10 in Auburn to I-290 north to Worcester and then to I-190 north to exit 5. Take State 140 north nine miles to Mountain Road.
Hours: Trails open daily sunrise to sunset. Visitors center open daily 9:00 A.M. to 4:00 P.M.
Pets: Allowed.
Best time to visit: Year-round.
Activities: Hiking, biking, picnicking, mountain bike riding permitted on paved and gravel roads, cross-country skiing, snowshoeing, snowmobiling, downhill skiing at adjacent Wachusett Mountain ski area.
Other: Wachusett Meadow Wildlife Sanctuary is southeast of the reservation. The Dickens Trail connects the two. The sanctuary contains eleven miles of trails.
For more information:
    Wachusett Mountain State Reservation, Mountain Road, Princeton, MA 01541; 508-464-2987 and 508-464-2712.

TOWER HILL BOTANIC GARDEN

While the first of January marks the start of another calendar year, mid-April is the unofficial beginning of another year at Tower Hill Botanic Garden.

That's when hundreds of flowers begin to bloom, filling the air with intoxicating fragrances and dressing up the grounds in a multitude of colors. After a harsh New England winter, I found it a perfect place to welcome spring.

Three miles of walking trails wind through the 132 acres that sit atop Tower Hill, which rises 641.5 feet above sea level and offers sweeping views of Quabbin Reservoir and Mount Wachusett.

The pathways take visitors from manicured gardens to managed natural areas, which include meadows and a pond, to the Davenport Collection of 119 varieties of heirloom apples. The apple trees are worth a visit themselves. Many apples are the size of grapefruit.

The Worcester County Horticultural Society operates the gardens, which feature plants and trees that thrive in central New England.

The Stoddard Education and Visitors Center is a new addition. It's a place to visit first for an orientation and a map of the grounds.

Back outside, the lawn garden acts as a magnet. It contains over 300 varieties of trees and shrubs, plus the secret garden with its dizzying array of plants. Harbor mist, sun drops, dainty yellow moonbeam, purple bowman's root, fragrant jasmine, lilies, magnolias, and more are on display. Gardeners fuss over them.

The field, wildlife, and meadow gardens are left mostly in their natural state. The wildlife garden once was a dumping ground on Tower Hill farm. Now it's a nesting, feeding, and watering site for birds, bats, and

One of the apples in the Heirloom Collection

butterflies. Benches and a viewing station allow visitors to sit and observe wildlife. A steady stream of birds visit the feeders.

It's an ideal place to rest before the climb back up Tower Hill and the parking lot.

Where: From Boston take Massachusetts Turnpike west to I-495 north. Take exit 25 to I-290 west. Take exit 24 north. Follow Church Street north to French King Drive.
Hours: April to October, daily, 10:00 A.M. to 5:00 P.M. November to March, weekdays, 10:00 A.M. to 5:00 P.M. Closes Thanksgiving, Christmas, and New Year's.
Admission: $3 for adults; $1 for children ages six to twelve.
Best time to visit: Spring to early fall.
Activities: Walk through 132 acres, active schedule of lectures and garden workshops, picnicking.
Pets: No.
For more information:
Tower Hill Botanic Garden, 11 French Drive, Boylston, MA 01505-1008; 508-869-6111.

PURGATORY CHASM STATE RESERVATION

Purgatory Chasm is a deep cleft, approximately sixty feet wide and a half-mile long. Sheer walls rise seventy feet on both sides of the boulder-strewn chasm floor.

Tall, stately hemlocks stand atop the cliffs, making the gorge seem even deeper. The coolness and shade bring relief on even the warmest day.

A blue-blazed trail starts at the southern end of the parking lot and leads through the gorge to the caves and hollows with names like Devil's Pulpit and Devil's Coffins. I scrambled through rocks, nooks, and crannies—a maze of geological wonders.

The chasm is a delightful and adventuresome place for children, who hoot and holler and play peek-a-boo among the rocks. All the work nature did to create the fault and series of fissures is of no concern to them. They just know the chasm is a lot of fun.

Just past the Devil's Coffin, which is the largest of the caves, the trail swings left and climbs out of the gorge. It runs along the top of the cliffs, where you can look down into the chasm below. The trail makes one final dip and turns to the parking lot.

Another choice for a walk is a yellow-blazed footpath that starts just past the picnic pavilion and makes a circuit through woodlands in the 2,660-acre reservation. It eventually swings past the far end of the gorge and ascends the cliffs on the western side of the chasm.

Where: From Massachusetts Turnpike take exit 10. Follow signs for State 20. Follow east to State 146 in Millbury. Follow State 146 south 7.5 miles to Purgatory Road. Follow one-half mile. Parking lot is on left.
Hours: Daily 8:00 A.M. to 8:30 P.M. Chasm is closed in winter. It opens in mid-April. Rest of park is open year-round.
Best time to visit: May through October.
Activities: Hiking, picnicking, hunting in season, cross-country skiing.

Pets: Allowed on leash.
For more information:
        Purgatory Chasm State Reservation, Purgatory
Road, Sutton, MA 01590; 508-234-3733.

DOUGLAS STATE FOREST/
CEDAR SWAMP TRAIL

Deep in the heart of the Douglas State Forest lies a well-kept secret — Cedar Swamp. There's little indication that the 4,555-acre forest is home to the swamp until one reaches the boardwalk that snakes through the wetland.

        To reach the half-mile Cedar Swamp Trail, walk past Wallum Lake, the picnic sites, bathhouses, and interpretive center. The red-blazed trail begins on the left a few feet past the center. Numbered markers correspond to those in a brochure available at the park headquarters.

        The first part of the trail lies in an area of mixed hardwood forest. The lesson learned here is how much adversity trees must endure, sometimes unsuccessfully.

        First is the tragic tale of the American chestnut. Once it dominated New England's deciduous forests, but that changed when the chestnut blight appeared in 1904 and eventually attacked nearly every stand of magnificent trees. The trail passes chestnut saplings, whose fate is sealed.

        What greets the visitor next are dead trees, victims of the gypsy moth. It is New England's most destructive pest, eating and stripping off leaves. Repeated attacks weaken trees and they die.

But enough of death and destruction. Cedar Swamp awaits. Going from the mixed hardwood forest into the swamp is like stepping from one's warm, sunny backyard into a cool, damp cellar.

The dense stands of Atlantic white cedar and hemlock trees allow little sunlight to reach the forest floor, where shade- and moisture-loving vegetation, such as sphagnum moss, thrives. The green, spongy moss holds many times its weight in water. Layers of dead sphagnum and sedge accumulate and form an organic deposit that is the source of peat moss widely used in gardening.

Skunk cabbage and cinnamon fern are bountiful as well. The cabbage in fact does smell skunky and the ferns are cinnamon-colored in the fall.

Cedar Swamp originated 10,000 to 15,000 years ago during the last Ice Age. After the glacier retreated, depressions were left behind and some became ponds or swamps. When the climate warmed, southern plants like American white cedar began to grow. Pockets of white cedar still survive in these swampy areas.

Where: Take Massachusetts Turnpike to exit 10. Follow I-395 south, then State 16 east for five miles. Follow signs.
Hours: Sunrise to sunset. Day-use areas open at 9:00 A.M.
Best time to visit: Year-round.
Pets: Allowed on leash.
Activities: Hiking, boating, canoeing, fishing, horseback riding, hunting in season, swimming, picnicking, cross-country skiing, snowmobiling, snowshoeing.

For more information:
Douglas State Forest, Wallum Lake Road, RR 01,
Box 161D30, Douglas, MA 01516; 508-476-7872

BLACKSTONE RIVER AND
CANAL HERITAGE STATE PARK

Sweet serenity. That was my state of mind as I stood atop
King Philip's Rock in Northbridge and watched Blackstone River ramble through the valley below. The large
stands of grass on the river's left were still in shadows
cast from trees on the eastern bank. But the mid-morning
sun shimmered on the water's surface.

It took only thirty minutes to walk the footpath
from the Blackstone River Heritage State Park Office
parking lot to the 408-foot-high King Philip's Rock,

A painted turtle taking the sun

which is named for the Wampanoag Indian chief. The promontory affords one of the finest views of the Blackstone River, a centerpiece of the state park that is maintained by the Massachusetts Department of Environmental Management.

Walking or canoeing are two of the best ways to enjoy Blackstone River and Canal. The Blackstone begins at the confluence of the Middle River and Mill Brook in downtown Worcester and ends forty-four miles south in Pawtucket, Rhode Island, where it becomes the tidal Seekonk River.

The entire stretch forms the Blackstone River Valley National Heritage Corridor. It highlights America's Age of Industry and Blackstone River's role in the revolution. Old factory buildings and machine relics from the steam-powered textile industry, begun in the 1790s, are found in mill towns throughout the corridor.

Today, Blackstone River and Canal are valued for their recreational uses. Along the meandering river are access points for canoeists and several trails, including the canal towpath.

A section of the towpath begins just west of the state park office and across a stone bridge over the Blackstone.

Head down Goat Hill Trails to the towpath and Rice City Pond. The small pond, named for the wild rice growing in it, is a favorite resting spot for migrating blackbirds in spring and fall.

Return to the stone bridge and follow the towpath south for two miles past Riverbend Farm to Stanley Wool Mill in downtown Uxbridge. The path is popular with strollers, dog walkers, bicyclists, and joggers.

Ducks and Canada geese are common, and you might see painted turtles sunning themselves.

Where: Hartford Avenue, Uxbridge. Take Massachusetts Turnpike to I-495 south to exit 20 in Milford. Take State 16 to Oak Street in Uxbridge and follow signs.
Best time to visit: Spring, summer, and fall.
Pets: Allowed.
Activities: Hiking, canoeing, picnicking, guided tours by National Park rangers.
Other: Just over the border from Massachusetts is Blackstone Gorge, just west of Slatersville. It provides one of the most scenic walks in the Blackstone River corridor. The gorge is one of the few remaining whitewater stretches on the river.
For more information:
Blackstone River Valley National Heritage Corridor Commission, 15 Mendon Street, Uxbridge, MA 01559; 508-278-9400. The commission supplies a free map and a Blackstone River Canoe Guide.

THE BUTTERFLY PLACE

Swallowtails, fritillaries, and milkweeds flitted among the plants before they alighted on their favorites to sip nectar and pollinate the vegetation process.

I soon was twisting and turning myself, trying to watch them all. I stopped mid-step as a red-spotted purple admiral landed on the sidewalk ahead. I ducked as a pair of cabbage whites headed straight for me.

I strained my neck to follow the flight of a stately monarch.

The butterflies inside The Butterfly Place at Papillon Park were surprisingly active, considering that outside the sky was gray and a light rain fell. Heat and light energize butterflies so they are most active on bright, sunny days.

Climate conditions inside The Butterfly Place closely resemble those of a greenhouse. A special heating system and artificial light do nature's work. The temperature is always at least seventy degrees Fahrenheit. The air is quite humid. Moisture fogs the glass walls and ceiling.

George Leslie and his wife Jane designed and created the 3,100-square-foot glass atrium. It is planted primarily with colorful flowering plants and shrubs to provide necessary nectar for the butterflies.

It contains as many as 500 butterflies representing forty species found mostly in North America. The types of butterflies on display change during the seven months that The Butterfly Place is open.

Every visitor can get a lesson in a butterfly's four life stages, or metamorphosis, from egg to caterpillar to pupa to adult pupa. Leslie delicately picked up a newly emerged butterfly, a zebra swallowtail, and hung it on a leaf before its first flight.

While some of the butterflies keep their distance, others are attracted to visitors. I bet the lady in front of me didn't know that a zebra longwing was resting on her left shoulder.

Where: The Butterfly Place is in Westford, approximately forty miles northwest of Boston. From I-495 take exit 32. Go north on Boston Road to Westford Center. At the Common, go right onto Lincoln Street to Main Street. Take Depot Street off Main Street. Cross State 40. Depot Street becomes Tyngsboro Road. The park is on the left in two miles.

Hours: Open daily, 10:00 A.M. to 5:00 P.M., mid-April through October.

Admission: $6 for adults; $5 for seniors sixty-five and over and children under twelve; free for children under three.

Best time to visit: Sunny days.

Activities: Butterfly observation, photography.

Other: A picnic area accessible to the handicapped is provided. There is a gift shop.

For more information:

   The Butterfly Place at Papillon Park, 120 Tyngsboro Road, Westford, MA 01886; 508-392-0955

WALDEN POND STATE RESERVATION

Walden Pond State Reservation in Concord presents the visitor with two very different experiences. One centers around Walden Pond and the recreational activities it offers. The second is more serene and involves the surrounding woodlands and the site of the one-room cabin where American writer and naturalist Henry David Thoreau lived for two years from 1845 to 1847. Thoreau immortalized the pond and the forest in the book *Walden,* which was based on the journal he kept during his stay.

But on a hot August afternoon the water beckoned. Walden Pond is popular with boaters (only canoes and nonmotorized boats are allowed). Some try their luck for rainbow trout, smallmouth bass, or perch.

Bathers flock to the small beaches. Red Cross Beach on the north shore is just a narrow strip of sand. The larger Main Beach, bathhouse, and concession stand are on the south shore. So is the boat launch at Deep Cove.

Even with the number of visitors limited to 1,000 at a time, the beaches are often cramped. In search of a little elbow room, I followed Pond Path past Red Cross Beach and Thoreau's Cove to the far end of the pond, to Ice Fort Cove and Long Cove. Both provided escape from the crowds.

I decided to sit and rest awhile. With the din of the crowd across the pond muffled, I became aware of other sounds. Water lapping the shoreline, birds singing, squirrels and chipmunks chattering in the trees behind me.

Much of Walden's forest had been cut down before the state acquired the property in 1922. The woods have since grown back with hickory, oak, and pines. They attract chickadees, blackbirds, kingfishers, and red-tailed hawks.

The pond was pristine. A pamphlet I had obtained at the park headquarters explained that this is due to the lack of shoreline development and tributary streams that carry decayed leaves, dirt, and other debris. Walden's water level rises and falls more slowly than most other ponds because it intersects the water table, making it less affected by wet and dry spells.

Monarch butterflies migrate from Mexico to Massachusetts

Like many ponds in Massachusetts, Walden's beginning dates back 10,000 to 12,000 years to the retreat of the glacier that covered New England. Walden is a kettlehole, a steep hollow left behind when an ice block melted.

To complete my visit, a stop at Thoreau's cabin site was in order. Woods Path leads to the spot where Roland Wells Robbins, an amateur historian, discovered and excavated the foundation of the cabin's chimney in 1945. The National Park Service designated Walden Pond as a Registered National Historic Landmark in 1965.

Thoreau lived at Walden Pond from July 4, 1845, to September 1847. His time was spent keeping a journal, studying nature, gardening, surveying the pond, and drafting his book *A Week on the Concord and Merrimack Rivers.*

I found myself trying to imagine what it was like 250 years ago during Thoreau's sojourn. The reservation is worth a visit for no other reason than the one Thoreau gave: ". . . my friends ask me what I will do when I get there. Will it not be employment enough to watch the progress of the season?"

Where: From Boston take State 2 west to State 126 (Walden Street). Follow south for four miles. Entrance to parking lot is on left. From Massachusetts Turnpike take I-495 north to State 2. Follow west to State 126 and go four miles to entrance.

Hours: Daily, 5:00 A.M. to sunset. The park is closed when it reaches 1,000 capacity. A time for reopening is posted at entry points. Parking fee.

Best time to visit: Year-round.

Pets: No.

Activities: Swimming, walking, picnicking, canoeing, fishing, cross-country skiing. Interpreters offer guided and educational tours, and staff the replica of Thoreau's cabin.

GLACIAL LANDSCAPE

A kettle pond such as Walden Pond is among the geological features formed when the last glacier slowly swept across New England 15,000 years ago and then gradually retreated 10,000 to 12,000 years ago as the climate warmed.

The face of the bedrock hills was changed. Ice erosion caused smooth surfaces on the north side and jagged ones on the south side where bedrock was torn off.

Large boulders broke off along joint lines where freezing and thawing occurred. These rocks were carried in glacial water and scattered, sometimes ending up miles from where they were plucked up. These boulders are known as glacial erratics. Many are found on Cape Ann in northeast Massachusetts.

Narrow ridges of sand, gravel, and boulders are eskers. They resulted from glacial streams running through ice tunnels.

Rounded hills known as drumlins are common in Massachusetts. They are deposits of glacial till, a mixture of debris consisting of clay, sand, and broken rocks. World's End Reservation in Hingham contains excellent examples.

Cape Cod is dotted with kettle ponds. The depressions were formed when a mass of ice separated from the glacier and was covered with debris. When the ice melted, the depression was formed. Where the water table is near the surface the depressions filled with water and became ponds.

Lake Hitchcock normally is mentioned when glaciers are discussed. Debris from the retreating glacier piled up in a central Connecticut valley, forming a dam and blocking the path of glacial rivers. The waters backed up and formed Lake Hitchcock, which extended 180 miles from Middletown Connecticut, through Massachusetts to northern Vermont.

When the dam broke, the Connecticut River cut a path through what was the lake floor.

For more information:
Walden Pond State Reservation, State 126, Concord, MA 01742; 508-369-3254.

GREAT MEADOWS
NATIONAL WILDLIFE REFUGE

With temperatures topping ninety degrees Fahrenheit and humid air hanging heavy, the great blue heron was content to loaf in the shallow water along the edge of the large marsh pool. No need to exert itself.

Three canoeists apparently felt the same way. After hauling their canoes out by the sleepy Concord River, they were enjoying a picnic lunch on the grass adjacent the Dike Trail, seemingly unaware of the magnificent bird strolling in the water on the other side of the knoll.

The handful of birdwatchers were a bit more energetic. They walked alone or in pairs along the 1.7-mile circuit trail, raising their binoculars from time to time to scour the freshwater wetlands. I did the same and spotted another great blue heron. This one was diligently searching for food.

Two units form the 3,000-acre Great Meadows Wildlife Refuge: the Dike Trail Area in Concord and the Weir Hill Area in neighboring Sudbury. Weir Hill contains the refuge office, visitors center, and educational facilities.

Concord River flanks the Dike Trail Area, while Sudbury River runs past Weir Hill Area.

The refuge is twenty miles west of Boston and just a few miles from Walden Pond State Reservation.

Native Americans once lived off the rivers and surrounding land. According to National Wildlife Refuge officials, "Great River Meadows" was the name settlers gave the grasslands left behind each summer by the rivers' retreat.

Over 200 species of birds have been recorded at the refuge. Waterfowl, wading birds, and other migratory birds rest and feed in the refuge. Wood ducks, black ducks, and mallards nest in the freshwater wetlands.

So does Blanding's turtle. Seeing one is a special treat because the turtle is rare in Massachusetts.

Chances are better that you might see a white-tailed deer. Muskrats, foxes, raccoons, cottontail rabbits, and weasels are common.

Where: To Concord Unit: from Boston take State 2 east to Concord. Turn right onto Main Street and go one block. Take State 62 east 1.3 miles. Turn left on Monsen Road and follow signs to refuge.

To Sudbury Unit: from Boston take State 20 west to Wayland. At light, turn right on State 126/27 and then bear left on State 27 north. Turn right onto Water Row Road and then onto Lincoln Road. Turn left onto Weir Hill Road.

Hours: Grounds open daily sunrise to sunset. Visitors

center at Sudbury Unit, 8:00 A.M. to 4:00 P.M., Monday to Friday, year-round; 11:00 A.M. to 5:00 P.M., Saturday and Sunday, May through October.

Pets: Allowed on leash.

Best time to visit: Spring and fall bird migrations.

Activities: Hiking, birdwatching, photography, cross-country skiing. Canoeing and fishing in Concord and Sudbury Rivers.

For more information:

Great Meadows National Wildlife Refuge, Weir Hill Road, Sudbury, MA 01776; 508-443-4661.

3

Eastern
Massachusetts

GARDEN IN THE WOODS

Delightful Virginia bluebells, bloodroots, and trout lilies usher in the spring at Garden in the Woods in Framingham. They are among the first to bloom

Soon hundreds of others follow—shooting stars, great trilliums, yellow lady's slipper, wood phlox. They form a colorful mosaic along three miles of trails that wind through cultivated gardens and other botanic areas left in their natural state.

Later in the year, blue gentian, red cardinal, and violet asters end the garden's public season with a flourish.

Over 1,500 types of plants, including 200 rare and

endangered species, grow in the series of gardens that cover forty-five acres in the middle of suburbia. The majority of flora are North American.

Pink lady's slippers dot the hillside in the woodlands in June. I followed a footpath that runs alongside Hop Brook and rambles past skunk cabbage, ferns and spicebush, and winterberry before it ascends through a forest of maples, beeches, oak, white pines, and hemlocks.

The most delightful area centers around a rock garden and lily pond. Oconee bells, rare and endangered in North America, are found here. So is the Labrador violet, a rarity in New England.

Northeast plants dominate, but the gardens also display plants from other temperate regions in North America, Europe, and Asia. Each plant is labeled, and color-coded signs indicate what ones are rare or endangered.

New England Wild Flower Society owns and operates the gardens, which open to the public from mid-April through October. Landscape designer Will C. Curtis and partner Howard Stiles designed and developed the garden for thirty-four years from 1931 to 1964, when the New England Wild Flower Society became the overseer.

Visits are rewarding anytime. The diversity of plants guarantees that blossoms are always plentiful.

Where: From north, south, and east take State 128 to State 20 west. Go eight miles to Raond Road and follow Hemenway Road. From west take Massachusetts Turnpike to exit 12 and State 9 east. Follow to Edgell Road

Great trilliums or wakerobins bloom as robins arrive

exit. At end of exit take ramp, turn left onto Edgell Road, and follow to Water Street, then first left on Hemenway Road.

Hours: Trails are open April 15 to October 31, Tuesdays through Sundays, 9:00 A.M. to 5:00 P.M. Last admission to trails is one hour before closing. Closed Mondays except for Memorial Day.

Admission: $6 for adults; $5 for seniors sixty and over; $3 for children five to fifteen.

Best time to visit: April and May are peak time for spring flowers to bloom, but there are continuous displays through fall.

Pets: No.

Activities: Walking, botany study, garden tours, educational programs.

Other: New England Wild Flower Society operates a gift shop and sells plants.

For more information:

New England Wild Flower Society, Garden in the Woods, 180 Hemenway Road, Framingham MA 01071; 508-877-6574 for recorded information and events; 508-877-7630 for office.

PARKER RIVER NATIONAL WILDLIFE REFUGE/PLUM ISLAND

It didn't take long for Parker River National Wildlife Refuge to live up to its reputation as a premier birdwatching area.

I was bike riding on the narrow paved road through the refuge, less than a quarter-mile from the main gate, when I spotted a snowy egret standing amid the marsh grasses on the edge of Plum Island River. It was just a sneak preview of what was ahead.

The 4,660-acre refuge covers two thirds of Plum Island far up the northern coast of Massachusetts in Newburyport. The refuge serves as a resting and feeding area for migratory waterfowl, warblers, and shorebirds. During peak migrations in spring and fall, hundreds of ducks and Canada geese can blanket the sky.

Sandy Point Reservation at the island's southern point is a popular beach in the summer. The small parking lot often fills up by 8:00 A.M. and gates are closed. There are no lifeguards along the seven miles of unspoiled beach and the Atlantic Ocean's pounding surf.

I had brought my bicycle and rode from one end of the refuge to the other and back. A lot of people do the same.

Stop at the refuge's main gate to pay a small admission fee and obtain a trail map. Seven parking lots and boardwalks to the beachfront nature trails are located along the 6.5-mile road through the refuge. An observation tower at the far end of the parking area, Lot 7, provides an overview, taking in the ocean to the east and south and Broad Sound, Nelson Island, and hundreds of acres of salt marsh to the west and north.

Backtracking about 2.5 miles, one reaches Hellcat Swamp Nature Trail. A wide path leads to a manmade dike that separates two freshwater impoundments. You can climb an observation tower for a fine view. A great blue heron down below got a lot of attention. The lean, gray bird waded through water for quite some time before it took to flight, a magnificent sight.

Double back to the trailhead and follow Hellcat Swamp Nature Trail east. A boardwalk winds its way amid an assortment of shrubs and trees: black cherry, bayberry, birch, red maple, oak, pitch pine, fox grape. During my mid-September visit, many trees and shrubs displayed their lush fruit.

Midway on the trail the boardwalk swings into the open and there is a fine view of the beach dunes. Bird-watchers gather here. The boardwalk then swings left and returns to the starting point.

The best times to observe birds are early morning and evening. The sun was starting to set when I made Pine Trails my final stop. Mosquitoes were intense along the trail, but I stayed with it. My effort was rewarded when I saw the fringes of Broad Sound, a major feeding area for snowy egrets. I counted twenty of the lovely white birds. It was a fitting end to a wonderful visit.

Where: Take I-95 north to State 113 east. State 113 becomes State 1A in Newbury. Follow signs to Plum Island and Parker River Wildlife Refuge.
Admission: $5.
Hours: Sunrise to sunset. Visitor contact station is open daily 9:00 A.M. to 5:00 P.M. May through September.
Best time to visit: Year-round. Peak bird migrations occur in spring and fall.
Activities: Hiking, bicycling, birdwatching, swimming, hunting in restricted areas, surf fishing.
Pets: Allowed on leash October through April, but prohibited May through September.
Other: Portions of the beach are closed April 1 through August 3 to protect nesting birds (piping plovers and least terns).

For more information:
Parker River National Wildlife Refuge, Northern Boulevard-Plum Island, Newburyport, MA 01950; 508-465-5753.

IPSWICH RIVER WILDLIFE SANCTUARY

It was only fitting to arrive at Ipswich River Wildlife Sanctuary in Topsfield by canoe.

There are twenty-two canoe access points along the thirty-one-mile stretch of the Ipswich River from Wilmington east to the Atlantic Ocean. One is on the eight-mile stretch of the river that snakes along the southern end of the sanctuary.

My partner and I glided our canoe through open marshes and wooded swamps. With so many cattails and sedges along the river's edge, it wasn't a surprise to see a muskrat swimming off the canoe's port side.

Any canoeist who stops at the sanctuary and wants to walk its trails should head up to the office and pay a small admission fee first. The Massachusetts Audubon Society owns the 2,800-acre sanctuary, the largest in the statewide system. Ten miles of trails loop through meadows, islands, and a manmade rockery.

Sanctuary headquarters sits atop Bradstreet Hill, which is actually a drumlin or glacial drift.

The observation tower overlooking Bunker Meadow is a prime spot for observing waterfowl that rest and feed in the meadow. There was little bird activity on the warm

A muskrat along the shore

afternoon in June. Early morning or evening are better times to visit the tower.

The rockery is a delightful place to visit any time of the day. It is a particular favorite of children, who zig-zag through the maze of boulders on the edge of Rockery Pond. The half-mile Rockery Trail begins behind sanctuary headquarters and heads downhill to the pond. Colorful and fragrant mountain laurel and azalea were in full bloom.

A previous owner of the property, Thomas Procter, imported many of the flora that line Rockery Pond and hired a landscape architect to design the rockery. The top of the grotto looks across the picturesque pond.

Another area worth a visit is Averill's Island. A 1.2-mile trail loops around the island. It begins just past Waterfowl Pond. White pine, beech, and hemlock dominate the woodlands.

Where: Take I-95 north to State 1 north. Take State 97 south at traffic light. Take second left off Perkins Row. Sanctuary is one mile on right.

Hours: Grounds open dawn to dusk. Closed Mondays except major holidays.

Admission: $3 for adults; $2 for senior citizens and children; free for Massachusetts Audubon Society members.

Best time to visit: Year-round.

Activities: Hiking, birdwatching, canoeing, educational programs.

Pets: No.

Other: Canoe and cabin rental (Innermost House) and

camping on Perkins Island are available to Massachusetts Audubon Society Members.

For more information:

Ipswich River Wildlife Sanctuary, 87 Perkins Row,
Topsfield, MA 01983; 508-887-9264.

MIDDLESEX FELLS RESERVATION

Middlesex Fells Reservation is a 2,060-acre preserve of
woodland, seven miles north of downtown Boston. The
Metropolitan District Commission manages the reservation and the nearby Walter D. Stone Memorial Zoo.

Sights and sounds of a major metropolis mingle
with those of the forest. Cars and trucks speed up and
down I-93, a north-south throughway that splits the
reservation into two sections. During my visit, one plane
after another flew over as they approached Logan International Airport. One minute an airliner overhead was
heard. The next minute the chirping of crickets and frogs
at Bellevue took its place.

"Fells" is the Saxon word for rocky, hilly terrain.
The reservation is aptly named.

A walk up 243-foot Pine Hill and its stone observation tower (a target of vandals) rewards the hiker
with a sweeping view of the Boston skyline and Boston
Basin.

Almost thirty miles of trails are found in Middlesex
Fells Reservation. Some are footpaths; others are old
carriage roads. The bridle paths are ideal for cross-
country skiing in winter. One footpath, the 4.3-mile

Cross Fells Trail, connects the reservation's eastern and western sections.

It took most of the afternoon to walk the Skyline Trail, which makes a 6.8-mile loop around the western section beginning at Bellevue Pond. It's a roller-coaster walk up and down a series of small, rocky hills. Oak, red maple, and hickory dominate the woodlands.

On a dry, hot summer day the Reservoir Trail beckoned as a side trip. It runs just outside a buffer zone for a string of reservoirs owned by the town of Winchester. I knew the trail was a good choice when a refreshing breeze blew across the water.

Some visitors drive to an area known as Sheepfold. It's an open, grassy knoll with ample room for kite flying and picnicking.

The reservation's eastern section is more rugged. The four-mile Rock Circuit Trail and connector trails traverse several short but steep ascents to rocky knobs. The Black Rock Section is particularly rugged.

Where: From Boston take I-93 north to exit 7 for State 28 and Fellsway West. Go left over the expressway and then right for South Border Road. Parking area is next to Bellevue Pond. From State 128 north of Boston take exit 37A to I-93 south. Follow 4.8 miles to exit 7 and State 28 and Fellsway. Follow as above.

Hours: Daily sunrise to sunset.

Best time to visit: Year-round.

Activities: Hiking, picnicking, horseback riding, fishing, bicycling in designated areas, cross-country skiing.

Friends of Middlesex Reservation sponsor hikes and natural history programs.

Pets: Allowed on leash.

For more information:
Middlesex Fells Reservation, c/o CANEPI, Woodland Road, Stoneham, MA 02180; 617-662-5142. Friends of Middlesex Reservations, c/o CANEPI, 28 Henry Street, Arlington, MA 02174. Detailed maps are available from both for a nominal fee.

WALTER J. STONE MEMORIAL ZOO

Stone Memorial Zoo is up the road from Middlesex Fells Reservation. The Metropolitan District Commission manages the zoo, whose exhibits are undergoing major upgrading.

The zoo's rebirth is exemplified by the newborn animals, a llama and a mouflon.

The renovated wetlands exhibit and artificial pond is home to geese, ducks, ferns, cattails, and water lilies. Other exhibit areas are northern forest, tropical forest, grasslands, polar bear tundra, and giraffe house.

The main feature of the enclosed tropical forest is an aviary with sixty birds representing fifteen species. Exotic birds such as Victoria crown bluebirds, Lady Ross turaco, and imperial fruit pigeon entertain visitors.

Outside, the resident polar bear apparently decided the August afternoon was too hot for anything but snoozing in the shade.

The heat didn't faze other animals. Graceful American flamingos perched on one leg, then the other. Colobus monkeys chattered and jumped from one place to another.

And the capybara scurried around. What is a capybara I wanted to know. It's only the largest rodent in the world. A native of Brazil, the capybara can grow four feet long and twenty inches high and weigh 150 pounds.

After reading that bit of information, I quickly headed for the giraffe house.

Where: Pond Street, Stoneham. Follow signs off I-93.
Hours: Daily, 10:00 A.M. to 4:00 P.M. Closed weekends in the winter.
Admission: $2 for ages twelve and up; $1 for children four to eleven years, seniors, students, and military personnel.
Pets: No.
Activities: Animal observation, special exhibits, and events.
Other: Concession stand.
For more information:
617-442-4896.

NEW ENGLAND AQUARIUM

It's feeding time for the marine life in the Giant Ocean Tank. Two divers clad in wet suits check their air tanks one more time, adjust their goggles, grab their bags of food, and slip into the waters of the 180,000-gallon tank.

More than 800 specimens of aquatic life reside in the tank, which is the centerpiece of the New England Aquarium in Boston. Sharks, sea turtles, moray eels, and tropical fish are among the dwellers.

The tank, filled with filtered water from Boston Harbor, spirals nearly to the ceiling. A coral reef in the center rises four stories high. The reef looks real, but it is made of fiberglass corals and sponges. The marine life like it anyway.

The divers feed and check the tank's occupants as they slowly make their way downward. The routine is repeated several times a day — the aquarium's population consumes about 125,000 pounds of fish a year.

As the divers did their work, visitors gathered around the tank, looking through glass windows and listening to a staff member on the other side provide commentary about marine life. One learns that the moray eel looks dangerous but it rarely attacks unless provoked; that an active sea turtle must come to the surface to breathe every five to fifteen minutes but can remain under water for three hours when it sleeps.

A visit to the aquarium is a learning experience. Sea lion presentations on board *Discovery* are entertaining, but they also increase public awareness of the environmental hazards the large mammals face. Plastic is a prime culprit. It can entangle and choke them.

The harbor seals that sun themselves seem carefree. But nearly all survived harrowing experiences as pups. Many were found injured or abandoned on New England

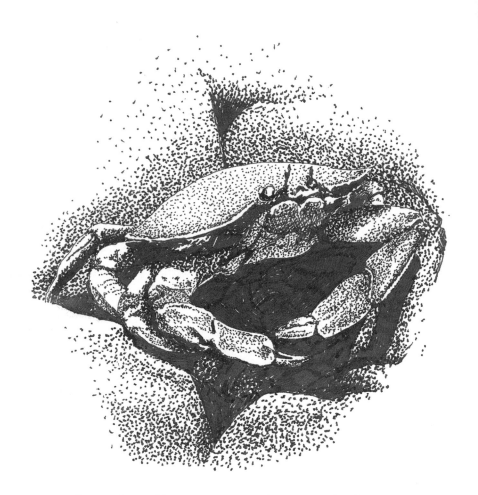

Face to face with a crustacean at the New England Aquarium

beaches. The aquarium helps rescue and rehabilitate
them. Many are later released to the sea. Some find new
homes in zoos and other aquariums.

The aquarium contains ten galleries. In the Edge of
the Sea Gallery visitors are encouraged to pick up and

touch horseshoe crabs, sea urchins, and other animals found in a typical New England tide pool.

Some of the aquarium's residents raise quite a ruckus. The penguins, of the jackass and rockhopper variety, are quite boisterous. Jackass penguins have been at the aquarium since it opened in 1969. The first ones were brought from islands off South America. They have given birth to twenty-two chicks over the years.

Where: Central Wharf. From Southeast Expressway (State 3) traveling north, take exit at Atlantic Avenue; traveling south take exit at Dock Square/Callahan Tunnel, pass under expressway and follow fish logo signs to aquarium. By subway take the Blue Line to Aquarium Stop.

Hours: Labor Day-June 30, Monday through Wednesday, 9:00 A.M. to 5:00 P.M.; Thursday, 9:00 A.M. to 8:00 P.M; Friday, 9:00 A.M. to 5:00 P.M.; Saturday, Sunday, holidays, 9:00 A.M. to 6:00 P.M. July 1–August 31, Monday, Tuesday, Friday, 9:00 A.M. to 6:00 P.M.; Wednesday, Thursday, 9:00 A.M. to 8:00 P.M.; Saturday, Sunday, holidays, 9:00 A.M. to 7:00 P.M. Admission fee.

Best time to visit: Year-round.

Activities: Marine wildlife exhibits, sea lion presentations, harbor tours (March to December) offer hands-on sampling and water testing in Boston Harbor.

For more information:

New England Aquarium, Central Wharf, Boston, MA 02110-3399; 617-973-5200. Harbor tour reservations: 617-973-5207.

BOSTON HARBOR ISLANDS STATE PARK

Strolling through the woodlands on Peddocks Island, one seems far removed from the bustle of metropolitan Boston. But, in fact, the island is just a quarter-mile off-shore from Hull and Nantasket Peninsula.

It seemed even more unimaginable at night, when looking up at the stars while sitting beside my well-weathered tent. Every so often, an incoming flight to Logan International Airport across the way disturbed tranquility.

Peddocks and neighboring islands comprise Boston Harbor Islands State Park. Some islands, like Peddocks, Georges, and Lovells, come under the jurisdiction of the Metropolitan District Commission. Others, like Gallops, Bumpkin, and Grape, are the responsibility of the Massachusetts Department of Environmental Management.

Twenty-seven islands dot Boston's inner and outer harbors. Some are little more than piles of rocks while others contain trails, campsites, and remains of old forts, a throwback to a time when the islands were active in the harbor's defense.

Ferry service to Georges Island is available from Long Wharf near the New England Aquarium, Hingham Ship Yard, and Lynn Heritage Park. A free water taxi can be taken from Georges to the other islands on a seasonal basis, weather permitting.

Camping is allowed at Lovells, Peddocks, Bumpkin, Calf, Grape, and Great Brewster.

Georges Island is in the far reaches of the Outer Harbor, a forty-five-minute boat ride from Long Wharf.

The view west from the island is of the spectacular Boston skyline. The view east is of the open Atlantic Ocean.

Fort Warren, a National Historic Landmark, is located at the center of the twenty-eight-acre island. The fort was first used as a prison for captured Confederate soldiers during the Civil War. Peering into dark, dirt-floored rooms in the fort's remains, one shivers at the thought of living here.

Peddocks Island, in Inner Harbor, is rich in military history as well. Fort Andrews was active from 1904 through World War II. The fort's old brick buildings and gun batteries remain. The 134-acre island is one of the largest in the harbor. For a pleasant walk, follow a trail west of the boat dock. It eventually goes along a salt marsh and reaches a wildlife sanctuary on the island's west end. Peddocks Island Trust and the Appalachian Mountain Club sponsor activities on the island.

Lovells Island is just minutes away from Georges Island via water taxi. It too contains remnants of a military installation. Fort Standish was built in 1900 and was active through World War II. The sixty-two-acre island quickly became my favorite. Its position near the edge of the Outer Harbor and the Atlantic Ocean makes it relatively remote and wild, particularly along the hilly northern end. Marshes and woodlands attract a variety of birds.

Camping is available near the Fort Standish remnants and south boat ramp. It's the only island with a designated swimming beach. Migratory shorebirds and other waterfowl are attracted to the island's marshes, woodlands, and ocean edges. Canada geese and sea ducks are plentiful. Pink and white campion, fragrant saltspray rose, and English plantain are scattered throughout the islands.

Where: Ferries to Georges Island leave from Long Wharf and Rowes Wharf near the New England Aquarium on Boston's central harborfront. From the north take exit 24 (Callahan Tunnel) off I-93. Proceed across intersection to parking. From the south take exit 22 (Atlantic Avenue–Northern Avenue) off I-93. Parking is straight ahead.

Public transportation, take Massachusetts Bay Transit Authority Blue Line to Aquarium Stop.

Hours: Ferries operate daily 9:00 A.M. to 5:00 P.M. May through October. Bay State Cruises, 617-723-7800; Boston Harbor Cruises, 617-227-4321; and Massachusetts Bay Line, 617-749-4500 provide service to Georges Island.

Admission: Rates vary among the commercial boats. Seasonal taxi service from Georges Island to other islands is free.

Best time to visit: Late spring to early fall.

Activities: Walking, camping (with permit), fishing, boating, nature study, historic study. Park rangers and volunteers offer island walks and fort tours.

Pets: No.

For more information:

Boston Harbor Islands State Park, Building 45, 349 Lincoln Street, Hingham, MA 02043; 617-523-8386.

EMERALD NECKLACE

Emerald Necklace is a string of nine continuous parks in the heart of Boston. They start with the Boston Common and the Public Garden and end with Franklin Park Zoo. Jamaica Pond and Arnold Arboretum lie between them.

Other components are Commonwealth Avenue Mall, a thirty-two-acre promenade lined with linden, green ash, and maple; Back Bay Fens, with community gardens and a rose garden; the Riverway, a linear park along the Muddy River with a foot and bicycle pathway; Olmsted Park, a heavily wooded park with Leverett's Pond and Ward's Pond, and a kettlehole surrounded by a pathway, boathouse, and bandstand.

Famed landscape architect Frederick Law Olmsted designed all but three of the parks. He designed the park system in the nineteenth century, creating green spaces for transportation corridors, respites from city noise and pollution, and recreational purposes. Today, the parks are listed in the National Register of Historic Places.

You can walk from one end to the other, but it's a long haul — fifteen miles. A better way is to visit one or two places during an outing. Here are the ones highly recommended.

Boston Common/Public Garden

Created in 1634, Boston Common is the grand dame of America's parks. Cows once grazed here and Colonial

**Frederick Law Olmsted designed the park system
in the nineteenth century**

militia gathered for the Revolution. It still is a public forum.

Across the street is the Public Garden. I did what thousands of visitors do. I took a swan boat ride. They operate daily 10:00 A.M. to 4:00 P.M. mid-April to late September.

Wide, paved pathways go past colorful flower beds and shady trees. Some species are imported, like the Maidenhair and dawn redwood from China, the Thurlow weeping willow from Japan, and the Belgian elm.

Arnold Arboretum

Approximately 15,000 trees, shrubs, and vines grow at Arnold Arboretum. Expect to spend several hours walking the 265 acres. The casual visitor, like myself, will simply enjoy looking at the common oaks, mountain laurel, conifers, English ivy, and midwinter euonymus from Northern China. The serious botanist can do a lot of studying. Each tree and plant has been scientifically researched and documented. Metal plates with common and scientific names are attached to each one.

The arboretum was founded in 1872. Harvard University leases the land from the city and manages the collection of plant life.

All the trees here are from the northern temperate zone. The hardy plants can withstand New England's changing weather conditions, the summer's heat and humidity, and winter's harsh winds, cold, ice, and snow.

You'll probably want to return throughout the year, as every season offers delightful scenery. Shadbush, redbud, and dogwood are among the first to bloom in the spring. Then it's mountain laurel, rhododendrons, and lilacs. As late as November, varieties of euonymus display delicate pink blossoms.

Climbs to 198-foot Bussey Hill and 235-foot Peters Hill offer sweeping views of the grounds below.

The trees and shrubs make ideal shelters for a variety of birds, while cones and berries provide them with a ready food supply. Squirrels and chipmunks feast on abundant acorns from oak trees.

It's a dizzying effort to find one tree or shrub that stands out. Traipsing through the arboretum in late November, I thought I found that special one on the northern slope of Peters Hill—a Chinese Fringe with soft, blue berries.

But no, soon I discovered my new favorite—the glossy hawthorn, its branches weighed down with red berries resembling miniatures apples.

Then again, as I thought back to May and the lilac blossoms, I wasn't sure.

Franklin Park/Zoo

I couldn't help myself. I instinctively stepped back every time the Western gorilla charged forward and bounced off the glass enclosure. The highly protective gorilla did not like me looking at his female companion. The volunteer at Franklin Park Zoo's African Tropical Forest said it was common behavior. Only 35,000 Western lowland gorillas exist, all in wet, tropical forests like the one created at Franklin Park Zoo.

Chestnut-red Bongo antelopes, yellow-back duiker, West African dwarf crocodile, and leopard are some of the other occupants. Exotic birds fly overhead.

Zulu fig, bamboo, and Abyssinian banana are grown in the hot, moist conditions. The average temperature in a rainforest is 80 degrees Fahrenheit or more. Rainfall can exceed 400 inches a year. In comparison, average rainfall in Massachusetts is 41.5 inches.

The African Tropical Forest is the centerpiece of Franklin Park Zoo. But it's a lot more. Peacocks walk along the sidewalks and sit on railings outside Bird World.

I spent an entire afternoon here. Other attractions are the waterfowl pond, children's zoo, and Hooves and Horns exhibits.

Aoudad, aika deer, Grant's zebra, sable antelope, and Thomson's gazelle are among the year-round residents.

Beyond the zoo boundaries lie another 500 acres of Franklin Park. Trails lead past Scarboro Pond and through the Wilderness.

Where: Boston Common and Public Garden are downtown off Tremont Street, Boylston Street, and Park Street.

Arnold Arboretum is on the Arborway in Jamaica Plain. From Storrow Drive, follow the Fenway and State 1 south. There is only on-street parking. By public transportation take the Orange Line to Forest Hills and walk one block to Forest Hills gate entrance.

To reach Franklin Park follow State 203 east. Follow signs to enter park on Circuit Drive.

Hours: Swan boat rides, 10:00 A.M. to 4:00 P.M., daily mid-April to September. Arnold Arboretum Visitors Center, 10:00 A.M. to 4:00 P.M., Monday through Friday. Franklin Park Zoo, 9:00 A.M. to 5:00 P.M., daily year-round except for Thanksgiving, Christmas, and New Year's.

Best time to visit: Year-round.

Activities: Walking, botany study, swan boat rides, zoo, ranger-led tours, and educational programs.

Pets: Allowed on leash in certain parks.

For more information:

Boston Common Visitor Information Center is located on the Tremont side of the Common. It supplies maps and brochures.

Boston Parks and Recreation Department, 1010 Massachusetts Avenue, Boston, MA 02118; 617-635-4505. Commonwealth Zoological Corporation, 617-422-2002. Arnold Arboretum, 125 Arborway, Jamaica Plain, MA 02130; 617-524-1718.

BLUE HILLS RESERVATION

Blue Hills Reservation far exceeded my expectations. I'd read quite a lot about this sprawling woodlands thirty-five miles southwest of Boston. But the place still surprised me.

If possible, make separate trips to the eastern and western sections, and return again in winter to cross-country ski. You can even downhill ski on the William F. Rodgers ski slopes.

Over fifty miles of trails criss-cross the 6,500-acre reservation. Some are old carriage lanes and others are narrow footpaths over rugged terrain. The longest is the nine-mile Skyline Trail, which traverses the entire Blue Hills Range.

The Blue Hills are domes of granite. They originated when molten rock came up from the earth's interior, then cooled and solidified before it reached the surface.

My first trip was to the western section. Begin with a visit to the Blue Hills Trailside Museum. It's run by the Massachusetts Audubon Society for the Metropolitan District Commission, which oversees the reservation. It contains animal exhibits plus displays of the reservation's cultural and natural history. One learns that the Native Americans who lived in the area called themselves "Massachuseuck," meaning "people of the great hill."

I also learned that the reservation is home to the Timber rattlesnake, one of the rare and endangered species in Massachusetts. It probably was just as well I didn't find one during my travels.

The pond outside the museum attracts mallards, black ducks, and Canada geese. Water lily, pickerel weed, arrowheads, and blue flag grow here.

A well-worn footpath starts behind the museum and climbs moderately to Great Blue Hill. At 625 feet it is the highest point in the reservation. Eliot Tower, a stone observation post, affords sweeping views in every direction. The Boston skyline rises in the north. The reservation's Houghtons Pond lies to the south.

I took North Skyline Trail east, rambling up and down a series of hills, before it reaches park headquarters. South Skyline Trail is an alternate return route.

Other components of the western section are Houghtons Pond, a popular swimming area; Fowl Meadow, a large wetland along Neponset River that is a prime birdwatching area; Ponkapoag Pond, a fine fishing spot for pickerel and bass; and Ponkapoag Bog, where a boardwalk travels through a sphagnum moss mat and where osprey nest in dead trees.

During my outing to the eastern section I took the Skyline Trail to Chicatawbut Outlook. A second stone observation tower sits atop the outlook and provides another view of Boston and Boston Harbor.

I continued east along Skyline Trail as far as Kitchmakin Hill before I doubled back to the trailhead off State 28, the roadway that divides the reservation in two.

Rock climbers tackle crags in the Rattlesnake Hill area and steep walks in the twenty-two-acre Quincy Quarries Historic Site adjacent to the reservation. Vegetation changes as one hikes up and down the hills. You'll find oaks, maples, and hickories in one place; beech, hemlock, and yellow birch in another. Red cedar and pitch pine dominate certain others.

Where: Take State 128 south from Boston to exit 2B in Milton. Follow State 138 north for one mile to Blue Hills Trailside Museum.

Hours: Open year-round sunrise to sunset. Trailside Museum is open 10:00 A.M. to 5:00 P.M. Tuesday through Sunday and Monday, holidays. Nominal entrance fee.

Activities: Hiking, picnicking, swimming, fishing, boating at Ponkapoag Pond, rock climbing, mountain bike riding on designated trails, horseback riding, cross-country skiing, snowshoeing, downhill skiing, ranger-led interpretive programs.

Pets: Allowed on leash.

Other: Quincy Quarries Historic Site contains trails through the twenty-two acres that include Granite Railway Quarry. A small museum showcases the history of quarrying.

For more information:

   Metropolitan District Commission, South Region, 695 Hillside Street, Milton, MA 02186, 617-698-1802; Blue Hills Trailside Museum, 1904 Canton Avenue, Milton, MA 02186, 617-333-0690.

WORLD'S END RESERVATION

Taking in the magnificent view from Planter's Hill in World's End Reservation, one feels on top of the world. Planter's Hill is just 120 feet high, but it offers a sweeping vista of Boston Harbor and Boston Skyline. So does Rocky Neck, a fifty-foot-high cliff on the reservation's eastern side. It faces toward Boston's Outer Harbor and the Atlantic Ocean beyond.

   Trustees of Reservations oversees World's End, located on a peninsula that separates Hingham Bay and Weir River.

Several trails loop around the property. It took almost three hours to complete the walk from the parking lot to the far northern end and back. Benches are conveniently located along the broad, tree-lined pathways.

I visited in the fall, when the reservation is less crowded and foliage is splendid. Maple and oak trees in the woodlands en route to Planter's Hill put on a brilliant display of red and orange. They contrast with the deep green of Eastern red cedar.

I spotted a red-tailed hawk soaring above Planter's Hill and a great blue heron at the edge of a marsh. Migratory birds were sparse on this calm day, although they often are seen in goodly numbers in spring and fall. Two drumlins—one being Planter's Hill and the other being World's End—are connected by a narrow causeway. Drumlins are small hills formed of glacial drift over 10,000 years ago. The mostly oval-shaped mounds are common in southern New England.

On the other side of the causeway you pass a rocky beach and then head up World's End. After taking in the view, head back down and over the causeway. I took the path left to Rocky Neck, a high granite promontory.

The path runs past the manmade Ice Pond. At one time the pond was a valuable source of ice for farmers. Today, waterfowl find refuge in it. My approach startled a group of four mallards.

Once past the pond you can head straight back to the parking lot or take a short side trail to a boardwalk that goes through a marsh before you return to the main path.

Where: From Boston take State 3 south. Take exit 14 to

State 228 north. Go 6.7 miles and turn left on State 3A. Follow for one mile and turn right onto Summer Street. Cross Rockland Street at traffic light. Follow Martins Lane to entrance.

Hours: Open daily 10:00 A.M. to 5:00 P.M. in summer; 11:00 A.M. to 4:00 P.M. in winter. A small admission fee is charged.

Best time to visit: Spring to fall.

Pets: Allowed on leash.

For more information:

Trustees of Reservations, Greater Boston and Southeast Regional Office, 246B Washington Street, Canton, MA 02021; 617-821-2977.

4

Cape Cod

CAPE COD NATIONAL SEASHORE

Pristine beaches, magnificent dunes, pine and beech forests, freshwater ponds, and salt marshes accent Cape Cod National Seashore. The 1961 founding of the National Seashore protects the special qualities of the environment and habitats within its 44,596 acres. The forty-mile-long stretch between Eastham and Provincetown provides a variety of recreational activities. Swimming, fishing, bicycling, windsurfing, walking, and hunting are all possibilities.

Opportunities for historical study are plentiful. At Pilgrim Heights in North Truro is a spring thought to be the Pilgrims' first source of fresh water in America. Guglielmo Marconi built the first wireless station on the peninsula at Wellfleet.

Cape Cod has long inspired writers. Naturalist Henry Beston spent a year of solitude on Coast Guard Beach in 1927. His chronicle, *The Outermost House,* is a classic. Henry David Thoreau wrote of his journeys here in the 1850s in the book *Cape Cod.*

There are no accommodations or concessions on National Seashore property, but picnicking and camping in self-contained vehicles are allowed. Plenty of restaurants, motels, cottages, campgrounds, and bed and breakfast places are found in nearby towns.

You can see quite a bit in a weekend, but allow three to five days for a more leisurely and complete experience.

A Little Geology

Geologically speaking, the cape is young: it is a product of the Ice Age. Glaciers deposited rock, sand, and clay over the area 15,000 years ago. Glacial moraines, outwashes, and kettleholes are prominent features throughout the cape. State 6 through the cape follows the Sandwich moraine for a good distance.

Wind and water keep changing the cape, dissipating sand in some places, and building it up in others. Driving to Provincetown I passed sand dunes that are gradually encroaching on the roadway. Walking on Coast Guard Beach I passed areas where the parking lot once was.

Getting There

The National Seashore is located on what is known as the

Lower Cape, forty miles east of where Cape Cod begins. The Bourne and Sagamore Bridges over Cape Cod Canal unofficially mark your arrival on the cape.

Getting across the bridges and driving the roadways

Dunes, fences, and roses of Cape Cod

to the National Seashore can cause plenty of headaches just about every weekend in the summer. Sometimes, the trip back is far worse, with traffic backed up for miles on Sunday evenings. At one time Labor Day began the off-season, but now plenty of visitors come to the cape during the fall season to take advantage of lower prices and moderate temperatures.

You have three basic travel choices. They all merge in Orleans. The most direct and fastest way to reach the National Seashore is via State 6, a four-lane road part of the way. State 28 goes along the southern side of the cape. Traffic is often bumper to bumper; fast food restaurants and shopping plazas line both sides of the road for miles. The approach to Chatham is picturesque, however, and the final stretch to where State 28 meets State 6 in Orleans is one of the nicest on the cape. State 6A follows the north Cape Cod side and goes through towns with art galleries and craft shops. It too connects with State 6 in Orleans.

Where to Begin

Start with a visit to Salt Pond Visitor Center on State 6 in Eastham. Farther east is Province Lands Visitors Center on Race Point in Provincetown. Each contains exhibits, publications, audiovisual presentations, and information services. A busy schedule of ranger-led walks and interpretive programs are offered at both.

Salt Pond is open daily, mid-March to mid-January. It provides shuttle bus service to Coast Guard Beach, whcrc parking is limited. The shuttle runs from June to September. Province Lands is open daily mid-April to December.

In winter information services are available at Race Point Ranger Station in Provincetown and at park headquarters in South Wellfleet.

WALKING TRAILS

The National Seashore has nine self-guided nature trails. Leaflets are available at each trailhead. The Buttonbush Trail at Salt Pond Visitor Center has large text and Braille labels.

A note of caution. Poison ivy is abundant. Check for ticks after walks, especially if you've passed high grasses and bushes. Deer ticks can transmit Lyme disease, which can cause arthritis and meningitis if not detected and treated early.

Some of the trails are quite short. Cranberry Bog Trail, for instance, is just a half-mile long. But nice surprises often come in small packages. So it is in this case. The trail goes through Pamet Cranberry Bog. In June and July, the plant's pink flowers are in bloom. In September and October, the bright red berry appears.

Several other trails take their names from dominant vegetation found along the way. One is the 1.25-mile Atlantic White Cedar Swamp Trail which begins in Marconi State Site. I followed a boardwalk deep into the swamp and passed the strong-scented white cedar, either reddish brown or weathered ash gray in color. The swamp's layers of peat also support highbush blueberry, red maple, and swamp azalea. The difference from the habitat where the trail started was startling. There, soil was sandy and pitch pine and bear oak trees were stunted and contorted by howling winds.

Great Island Trail

By far the longest and most difficult trail in the National Seashore is Great Island Trail. It is four miles one way. There are some uphill climbs and stretches through sand. Take plenty of water, snacks, suntan lotion, and a hat. You'll be out in the elements for a long time.

It begins at the end of a deadend road in Wellfleet, three miles from State 6. The trail is poorly marked in places. More than once I found myself guessing which way to turn.

The beginning is easy enough to follow. It leaves from the parking lot and goes down a set of wooden stairs to an inlet of Herring River. High dunes separate the sandy path from Cape Cod Bay on the right. A marsh is on your left.

This stretch between the Wellfleet mainland and Great Island is known as The Gut. Soon the path swings left and continues around a marsh to a trail junction. You can proceed straight through a pitch pine forest, or turn left as I did and make a loop along the south side of the marsh. I had a field day picking up seashells, which is one of my favorite pastimes. I had quickly filled my pockets with colorful scallop shells. The brown shells of large horseshoe crabs were scattered on the beach.

Fifty minutes later I rejoined the main route. It leaves the pitch pines, skirts another marsh, and heads up Great Beach Hill. It's more pitch pines and yet another marsh before you reach tidal flats. I was lucky it was low tide. I could follow the sand flats across the narrow peninsula 1.5 miles to Jeremy Point. The area is under water during high tide. After a much needed break, I returned over the beach along Cape Cod Bay. With the soft sand underfoot, it took almost ninety minutes to reach the parking lot.

NATIONAL SEASHORE NATURE TRAILS

Eastham

Fort Hill Trail: 1.5 miles. Follow the sign off State 6 to Governor Prence Road. It overlooks Nauset Bay, goes through Red Maple Swamp, and passes remnants of Nauset Indian settlements and the former home of sea captain Edward Penniman (park rangers sometimes lead tours through the house).

Nauset Marsh Trail: one mile. Begin at Salt Pond Visitor Center. The trail goes past Salt Pond (a kettle pond) and a salt marsh, where you might see herons and other birds feeding on the rich food deposits brought by the high tide.

Buttonbush Trail: one-quarter mile. Begin at Salt Pond Visitor Center. The trail is specially designed for the visually impaired. There are guide ropes and signs with text in large print and Braille. It goes past a small kettle pond, black alder, and varieties of oak.

Wellfleet

Atlantic White Cedar Swamp Trail: 1.5 miles. Begin at Marconi Station Site. The trail passes through swamp with stately white cedars.

Great Island Trail: four miles one way. Begin at far end of Wellfleet Center. The trail travels through marshes and pitch pine forests. The final 1.5 miles goes over tidal flats along a narrow peninsula to Jeremy Point (impassable at high tide). Return over sandy beach along Cape Cod Bay.

Truro

Cranberry Bog Trail: one mile. Begin at Youth Hostel on North Pamet Road off State 6. Boardwalk goes through a cultivated cranberry bog.

Small Swamp Trail: three-quarters mile. Begin at Pilgrim Heights area. The trail goes through wooded area with pitch pine, bayberry, highbush blueberry, bear oak. Overlook to dunes called Peaked Hills. Here the British man-o-war *Somerset* grounded on Peaked Hills Bar on November 7, 1778.

Pilgrim Spring Trail: three-quarters mile. Begins at

Pilgrim Heights area. Leads to a site where Pilgrims may have discovered their first fresh water in New England in November 1620.

Provincetown

Beech Forest Trail: one mile off Race Point Road. The trail goes through a forest of American beech trees and loops around freshwater ponds. Other vegetation includes sheep laurel, swamp azalea, yellow birch, gray birch, black oak, and tupelo black gum. The trail is moderately difficult, going through soft sand and climbing up log steps.

BICYCLE TRAILS

The National Seashore contains nearly twelve miles of paved bicycle trails. The Nauset Trail is shortest at 1.6 miles. It goes between Salt Pond Visitor Center and Coast Guard Beach. Head of the Meadows Trail covers two miles between High Head Road at Pilgrim Heights in Truro to Head of the Meadows Beach.

It makes a lot of sense for the bicycle trails to take you to the beach. The beach was just the respite I needed after cycling the 5.75-mile loop trail and three spurs of the Province Land Trail. It's quite hilly with numerous twists and turns through dry, sandy land with lots of pitch pine.

The quarter-mile Race Point Road spur brings the

rider to Race Point Beach, while a one-mile path leads to Herring Cove Beach. My choice to head to Herring Cove was a good one. It was low tide, so I could walk far out along toward Long Point, the little hook of land at the top of the cape and the National Seashore.

The cape's relative flatness and well-maintained trail network makes bike riding a popular activity. The Cape Cod Rail Trail follows the right-of-way of the Pennsylvania Central Railroad nearly twenty miles from Dennis to Eastham. It connects Nickerson State Park with the Salt Pond Visitor Center. Free parking is available at the trail's access points.

Other recommended bike trails are Cape Cod Canal, which runs eight miles on both sides of the canal, and 3.6-mile Falmouth Shining Sea Trail, which goes between Falmouth and Woods Hole. The Shining Sea Trail is a personal favorite. It's straight, flat, and picturesque. Large maples and locusts line the path first. Then it passes marshes and goes along the beach in the direction of Nobska Light. It ends at Little Harbor in Woods Hole.

BEACHES

The nature walks and bicycle rides are part of the National Seashore experience, but what brings most visitors here are the beaches.

Cape Cod has 365 miles of shoreline, and arguably the most magnificent stretches are within the National Seashore. The parkland's beaches remain unspoiled despite their heavy use.

Everyone has a favorite. Mine is Race Point Beach, but you can't go wrong with any of the others—Nauset Light, Coast Guard, Marconi, Head of the Meadows, and Herring Cove. Several towns also have public beaches.

At Race Point, as at any other beach, you can walk for miles across pristine sand. You might see surf fishers trying to catch a supper of bluefish or striped bass. Charter boats are spotted at sea with passengers fishing the waters for cod, halibut, pollack, bluefin tuna, flounder, and sometimes haddock.

One day you might see a special treat as I did. The beach was fairly empty on an early October afternoon when I came across two fishermen peering through binoculars near Race Point Light. They had spotted a humpback whale a few hundred yards off shore. They were kind enough to let me take a look.

On my return large groups of herring gulls and great black-backed gulls walked the sand in front of me. A gannet dove repeatedly into the white-capped waves.

VEGETATION

The sandy soil that makes such beautiful beaches creates a fragile and impoverished environment for plants, shrubs, and trees. Ranger-led walks through Province Lands are a good way to learn about habitat that grows on the Outer Cape.

The booklet *Common Trailside Plants on the Cape Cod National Seashore* is a worthwhile purchase. I

The proud seagull

bought it at the Salt Pond Visitor Center and took it along on many of my excursions.

Pitch pines thrive in the poor glacial soils. Inland they can grow fifty feet tall, but salt spray and harsh winds stunt their growth in exposed areas. Black oak, white oak, sassafras, and black cherry are other common trees on the cape.

Despite their struggle for survival in the poor soil, some of the plants are quite beautiful. American beach grass is most conspicuous on cape dunes. Dusty miller has adapted to the harsh dune environment as well. Its yellow flowers first appear in July.

You'll also find broom crowberry, golden heather, beach pea, and beach heather. A little farther inland grow blueberry, huckleberry, and sheep laurel. Wet swamp areas support swamp azalea, winterberry, and highbush blueberry.

A ranger-led walk at Salt Pond took us on the edges of the marshes with their own array of plant life – the stringy eelgrass, glasswort, salt marsh hay, and sea lavender with its lovely purple flowers.

During calm, sun-drenched days in summer it seems that the dunes and their fragile plant life are out of harm's way. But a visit in late December when a rainstorm was bearing down on the cape changed my mind.

Wild surf pounds the shore. At high tide the waves reached the base of the high cliffs at Marconi Station Site. The cape's battle against erosion is a constant one.

Where: Take State 6 east across Cape Cod. The National Seashore begins on the Lower Cape forty miles east of Provincetown.

Hours: Trails and beaches for walking are open year-round dawn to dusk, Salt Pond Visitor Center is open daily, mid-April to December. Summer hours are 9:00 A.M. to 5:30 P.M. and winter hours are 9:00 A.M. to 4:30 P.M. Some evening programs are offered.

Admission: $5 parking fee at beaches.

Best time to visit: Year-round. Summer is peak tourist season. Fall is less crowded. Beaches and trails are always open, but lodging and other services outside the park are minimal in winter.

Activities: Walking, bike riding, swimming, picnicking, horseback riding on designated trails, fishing (state license required for freshwater fishing), interpretive programs, touring historic sites, overland vehicle sand use (April to November with permit, $45 a year permits operation of registered four-wheel-drive vehicle on designated routes, $75 a year to park overnight in designated areas April 15–November 15.

Pets: Allowed on leash in some places. Prohibited on nature trails, picnic areas, protected beaches.

Other: Gift shops at visitors centers, but no concessions. Charter fishing trips, whale watches, boat rentals, bike rentals, dune tours available throughout Cape Cod outside the National Seashore.

Life Saving Service and lighthouses have been an integral part of the cape. The Park Service conducts tours of the Old Harbor Life Saving Museum at Race Point Beach. Highland Light, Nauset Light, and Three Sisters Lighthouses are within the National Seashore.

Ferries leave Woods Hole and Hyannis for Martha's Vineyard and Nantucket. Good places to visit are Gay

Head Cliffs, Cedar Neck Tree Sanctuary, Felix Neck Wildlife Sanctuary and Cape Poge Wildlife Refuge on Martha's Vineyard, and Long Pond Sanctuary and Coskata-Coatue Wildlife Refuge on Nantucket. Some require a good deal of effort to reach.

The former whaling town of Provincetown is now a tourist mecca and art colony. Its main street blends sales of T-shirts, red plastic lobsters, and saltwater taffy with galleries for serious art aficionados. The town's famous landmark is Pilgrim Monument, which commemorates the landing of the Pilgrims in 1620 and the signing of the Mayflower Compact.

Golf rivals beach-going as a popular activity. The cape's golf courses are renowned.

For more information:

Superintendent, Cape Cod National Seashore, South Wellfleet, MA 02663; 508-349-3785. Salt Pond Visitor Center, 508-255-3421. Province Lands Visitor Center, 508-778-2600. Steamship Authority, P.O. Box 284, Department AA, Woods Hole, MA 02543; 508-540-2022

ASUMET HOLLY AND WILDLIFE SANCTUARY

Asumet Holly and Wildlife Sanctuary covers just forty-nine acres, but it contains a thousand holly trees. American, English, Chinese, and Japanese holly are represented among the eight species and sixty-five varieties.

It seemed a December visit was in order to this sanctuary whose fame comes in large part from holly. American holly's glossy green leaves and red berries are a favorite for Christmas decorations. In fact, the sanctuary holds Holly Days every December.

Holly lovers are forever indebted to Wilfred Wheeler, who was the state's first commissioner of agriculture and began the holly plantation in 1925. He selected Joseph Dias as superintendent. Together they chose and transplanted the best native American holly species based on their beauty and heartiness. The property was purchased by Joseph Lilly III after Wheeler's death. Lilly donated the preserve to the Massachusetts Audubon Society in 1964.

A trail map and pamphlet highlighting fifty-one hollies are available at the sanctuary. Some of Asumet's hollies are full-size trees while others are shrubs three feet tall. Crossbreeding has led to varieties of blue hollies displayed at the sanctuary. One variety of Japanese holly has black berries, while one American holly transplanted from nearby Barnstable has orange fruit.

My main interest was in the holly trees, but I soon discovered other features and put a summer visit on my schedule for next year.

One trail circles Grassy Pond, a kettle pond formed during the glacial retreat over 10,000 years ago. Lacking any brook, the pond is dependent on spring rainfall and its level fluctuates from year to year.

Rare wildflowers, including Plymouth gentian and sundew, grow in the pond habitat, which protects the rare damselfly. My visit was way past the best months to see the wildflowers, mid-July through September.

A short side trail goes past another kettle, this one a small bog where cranberries grow.

More than 130 bird species have been sighted at the

sanctuary. Each April since 1935 a colony of barn swallows has arrived. They mate and nest in an old barn at the sanctuary entrance. In August, the colony departs for its wintering grounds in the tropics.

Where: From State 128 and State 151 in North Falmouth, follow State 151 east for four miles. Turn right on Currier Road. Entrance is 100 yards ahead on right.
Hours: Grounds open dawn to dusk. Closed Mondays except major holidays.
Admission: $3 for adults, $2 for senior citizens and children. Free for Massachusetts Audubon Society members.
Best time to visit: Year-round.
Activities: Walking, bird and flower observation, natural history and horticultural programs, tours of Elizabeth Islands, Holly Days.
Pets: No.
Other: Lowell Holly Reservations in Mashpee has over 300 holly trees. Trustees of Reservations manages the 135 acres on a narrow peninsula, Conaumet Neck. Foot trails go to the tip of the peninsula and past two ponds.
     From State 6 take exit 2 and follow Route 130 south. Go left on Cotuit Road, then right on South Sandwich Road. Entrance is on right, hidden in woods.
For more information:
     Asumet Holly and Wildlife Sanctuary, 286 Ashumet Road, North Falmouth, MA 02536; 508-563-6390.

NICKERSON STATE PARK

It's easy to forget the natural aspects of Nickerson State Park during the summer, when campgrounds overflow, swimming areas teem with bathers, and cyclists ride the bike paths. But they are the reason Nickerson State Park is so popular. Nickerson contains eight kettle ponds, whose clean, refreshing waters attract swimmers, canoeists, and fishermen. And plenty of waterfowl.

The depressions were formed when the glacier retreated across New England thousands of years ago. In parts of Cape Cod where the water table is near the surface, the kettleholes became ponds. Cliff Pond is the largest one in Nickerson State Park. It seems to shrink in size during summer, when large crowds swarm the narrow, sandy shoreline.

Nickerson presents a different look in the late fall and winter. It's easy to walk the trails that encircle Cliff Pond, the smaller Little Cliff and Flax Ponds, and the even smaller Ruth Pond. Waterfowl are the primary occupants. So many times I came around a bend and startled either black ducks or mallards, who quickly took flight.

The narrow Little Cliff Pond is an excellent place for viewing waterfowl. Rows of cattails, arrowhead, and pickerelweed line its edges.

A bicycle is a good way to get around the 1,955-acre park. The three-mile Park Road Trail goes over rolling terrain past pitch pine, white pine, and spruce. Ruth Pond and Overlook Trails go through stands of stately red pines. The ride is moderately steep in places. You can connect with the twenty-mile-long Cape Cod Rail Trail outside the park entrance.

It took several attempts before I got a campsite for one stay in July. The 418 campsites had been available on a first-come, first-served basis, but the park planned to take reservations for the first time in 1994.

The park's main business is summer tourists, but winter enthusiasts are not forgotten. Bike paths serve as cross-country ski trails.

Where: Take State 6 east to exit 12 in Brewster. Take State 6A west and follow signs to entrance.
Hours: Day-use areas open dawn to dusk. Campgrounds open April 15 to mid-October. Cost is $6 a night for regular site and $7 for premium site on water's edge.
Best time to visit: Year-round.
Activities: Hiking, swimming, picnicking, camping, boating, fishing, horseback riding, cross-country skiing, ranger-led interpretive programs.
Pets: Allowed on leash.
Other: Camp store.
For more information:
Nickerson State Park, Main Street, Brewster, MA 02631; 508-896-3491.

MONOMOY NATIONAL WILDLIFE REFUGE

Trying hard to ignore the queasiness in my stomach, I popped another peppermint candy in my mouth and concentrated on the shoreline ahead as our small cruise boat pushed forward through choppy water and headed for the islands of Monomoy National Wildlife Refuge. We had left Outermost Harbor Marina in Chatham and were in search of harbor and gray seals who haul out on the winter beaches of North Monomoy Island and South Monomoy Island. I quickly forgot my discomfort when hundreds of harbor seals were spotted. They huddled in masses, covering entire sections of the shoreline.

The common small seals of brown and gray are well adapted to the frigid waters and air temperatures off Cape Cod and coastal waters as far north as Labrador. The large gray seal is sometimes seen on Cape Cod as well.

A harbor seal

I had signed up for the seal cruise through Wellfleet Bay Wildlife Sanctuary. The previous trips had been canceled because of stormy weather.

While seals are the primary attraction, plenty of waterbirds are seen. A variety of sea ducks—scooter, eider, oldsquaws—are abundant.

Most of the 2,750-acre refuge is accessible by boat only. The sanctuary and Cape Cod Museum of Natural History in Brewster offer day trips with naturalist guides to the 2.5-mile-long North Monomoy Island and the five-mile-long South Monomoy Island, which many consider the finest birdwatching spot in New England. The refuge provides nesting habitat to migratory waterfowl. Over 250 species have been observed at the refuge and forty-nine species nest here, including endangered piping plovers and roseate terns.

The forty-acre Morris Island section is accessible by foot and automobile over a dike connected to the mainland. Morris Island includes refuge headquarters and a 1.5-mile interpretive trail across beach, dunes, and salt marsh. A trail map and pamphlet on refuge birds is available at headquarters. The trail starts to the left of the building.

I took the trail during a visit in early September. Wooden steps lead down the cliffside to the beach below, where the trail heads west across the sand, then swings right toward a series of dunes. They are nesting grounds for herring gulls and black-backed gulls. The trail finally heads back to open Morris Island Flats, where sanderlings and gulls scurry about, picking at the sand each time a wave retreats. The trail follows the beach back to the wooden stairs and returns to the refuge parking lot.

COMMON SHOREBIRDS

The ocean beaches, tidal flats, and marshes in Massachusetts draw an assortment of birds. Here are some you may see:

Northern gannet: Frequently observed diving headfirst into the sea for food.

Common tern: It's the best-known tern in the East. It resembles a gull but is smaller, more slender, and with a more pointed bill.

Laughing gull: Just one of its species is found on Cape Cod. It is distinguished by dark feet, dark bill, gray back.

Sanderling: One of the more familiar sandpipers. A common sight on sandy beaches, it seems like it's always playing tag with the waves.

Piping plover: Prefers sandy beaches. Its nesting grounds are protected. The small, white bird has a black ring around its neck, black-tipped yellow bill, yellow legs and feet.

Greater yellowlegs: Mostly gray, with yellow legs. An early spring arrival.

Where: Take State 6 east to State 137 south to State 28 east through Chatham to Chatham Lighthouse and Coast Guard Station. Take first left after lighthouse, then first right. Follow Morris Island Road to signs for refuge on left.

Hours: Sunrise to sunset year-round.

Activities: Walking, birdwatching, seal watching, surf fishing, shellfishing (by permit).

Pets: No.

Other: Two organizations offer guided boat tours to Monomoy Islands. Cape Cod Museum of Natural

History in Brewster, 508-896-3867. Massachusetts Audubon Society, Wellfleet Bay Wildlife Sanctuary, 508-349-2615.

For more information:

Monomoy National Wildlife Refuge, Wiki Way, Chatham, MA 02633; 508-945-0594.

WELLFLEET BAY WILDLIFE SANCTUARY

Wellfleet Bay Wildlife Sanctuary provides a wonderful introduction to Cape Cod's habitats. Five miles of trails go past pine woods, ponds, fields, and salt marshes.

The fragrances of bayberry, sweet fern, and sweet pepperbush were delightful as I strolled Goose Pond Trail. A trail guide can be purchased at the sanctuary office for a nominal fee or can be borrowed for the outing.

The 1.5-mile self-guided nature trail goes through a woodland of pine and oaks to an earthen dam with Silver Spring Pond on the left and salt marsh on the right. During a summer visit yellow and white water lilies were in full bloom on the pond's surface. The trail then goes through a woodland of Norway spruce and various types of pine—scotch, pitch, red, white. The footpath soon reaches Goose Pond. The area attracts ducks, herons, kingfishers, greater yellowleg, least sandpipers, and semipalmated sandpipers.

Just beyond the pond a side trail can be taken to Try Island, unless high tide covers the boardwalk across the marsh. I was able to walk around the island and reach the tidal flats where shorebirds feed. The island is named after the early tryworks that rendered whale blubber into oil. Pilot whale bones have been found in the marsh over the years.

Double back to the junction with Goose Pond Trail. The pathway swings left past dainty dwarf wild rose, sea lavender, and beach grass. Soon after it rounds a bend, and the aromas of sweet fern, beach heather, and huckleberry fill the air. The trail eventually returns to Goose Pond and the path back to the sanctuary office.

On a return visit in early fall many trees and bushes sported bright foliage and held fruits that were colorful in their own right. Grapes are a particular favorite of birds. The beach plum comes in shades of reddish purple, blue, and yellow.

Where: Take State 6 east. Entrance is on left side of road immediately past Eastham-Wellfleet town line.
Hours: Grounds open winter 8:00 A.M. to dusk; summer 8:00 A.M. to 8:00 P.M.
Admission: $3 for adults; $2 for senior citizens and children. Free for Massachusetts Audubon Society members.
Best time to visit: Year-round.
Activities: Hiking, birdwatching, natural history programs, guided boat tours to Monomoy National Wildlife Refuge.
Pets: No.
Other: Nature center and gift shop. Family tent camping is available to Massachusetts Audubon Society members of at least one year.

For more information:
Wellfleet Bay Wildlife Sanctuary, Wellfleet, MA 02663; 508-349-2615.

WHALE WATCH

Nearly 1.5 miles out from Provincetown Harbor I was beginning to think my whale watch trip was a bust. Still no sighting. Many passengers, myself included, vainly scanned the water and horizon.

Moments later my worries ended when the captain eased up on the throttle as two whales were spotted at four o'clock high. They were humpback whales forty to fifty feet long. Humpbacks are resident whales of New England waters from mid-April through November. They winter in the West Indies.

The larger finback whale (fifty to seventy-five feet) is sometimes spotted. A special treat is the sighting of a right whale, because fewer than 350 North Atlantic right whales remain in the world. They can be seen in Cape Cod Bay in spring.

Five different humpbacks would capture our attention during the next two hours. Each time a whale was spotted, passengers scurried from starboard to port and back to watch the magnificent mammals.

I chose the Dolphin Fleet for my whale watch simply by happenstance. A discount coupon was available at the motel where I stayed the previous night. Several other companies offer whale excursions from Provincetown, Hyannis, Plymouth, and Boston. Most boats have open top decks, enclosed cabin concession stand, and restrooms.

Staff from the Center for Coastal Studies served as naturalists for the trip. The center conducts whale and

Take a boat out of Provincetown to watch whales

marine research. Researchers have followed many of the whales for years. They've assigned them names such as Salt, Trunk, and Agassiz.

Our spotters gleefully pointed out Salt, who was first sighted in cape waters in 1975. It was like running into a favorite family member. The whales are named and recognized by markings, particularly those on their dorsal fins. As one might suspect, the underside of Salt's dorsal fin was white.

I took one of the last whale watching trips of the season on the last Monday in October. The eighty or so passengers were told that whale activity had been quite high in the past few days. It was with much anticipation that we left the dock.

We slipped out of the harbor, past three small lighthouses, rounded Race Point, and headed into the open sea.

It took awhile to reach any whales, but once we did the action was practically nonstop. The first pair swam side by side before they dove under water, then surfaced a few minutes later, and let out a blow. I madly snapped photographs whenever a whale raised its fluke out of the water before diving back underneath the surface.

Two groups of ten to twelve Atlantic white-sided dolphins put on a show of their own. A couple of gannets were spotted as well.

Two humpbacks decided to get a closer look at us. First one, then the other, approached our vessel and swam underneath us a half-dozen times They were so close you could smell their foul breath. The naturalist called this a boat encounter. The climax came when a humpback breached, leaping completely out of the water.

There seemed to be no end to the whale sightings. Even though the captain extended our stay at sea, we headed back all too soon to Provincetown.

Where: Take State 6 east to Provincetown. Turn left onto Conwell Street, right onto Bradford Street, and left onto Standish Street. Pier is at end of street.

Hours: Most whale watching fleets operate daily April through October.

Admission: Rates range from $12 to $20 depending on age.

For more information:

In Provincetown, Dolphin Fleet, 800-826-9300; Provincetown Whale Watch, Inc., Ranger, 800-287-0374 in eastern Massachusetts only. In Plymouth, Capt. John Boats, 800-242-2469.

Selected
References

A Guide to the Properties of The Trustees of Reservations. The Trustees of Reservations (572 Essex Street, Beverly, MA 01915-1530), 1992.

Cruickshank, Allan D. *A Pocket Guide to Birds* (New York: Washington Square Press), 1960.

Friary, Ned, and Bendure, Glenda. *Walks and Rambles on Cape Cod and the Islands, A Naturalist's Hiking Guide* (Woodstock, VT: Backcountry Publications), 1992.

Jorgenson, Neil. *A Guide to New England's Landscape* (Chester, CT: The Globe Pequot Press), 1977.

Laubauch, Rene. *A Guide to Natural Places in the Berkshire Hills* (Stockbridge, MA: Berkshire House, Publishers), 1992.

Leahy, Christopher W. *An Introduction to Massachusetts Birds* (Lincoln, MA: Massachusetts Audubon Society), 1975.

Little, Richard D. *Exploring Franklin County, A Geology Guide* (Greenfield, MA: Valley Geology Publications), 1989.

Sammartino, Claudia F. *The Northfield Mountain Interpreter* (Berlin, CT: Northeast Utilities), 1981.

Stevens, Lauren R. *Hikes and Walks in the Berkshire Hills* (Stockbridge, MA: Berkshire House, Publishers), 1990.

Whatley, Michael E. *Common Trailside Plants of Cape Cod National Seashore* (Eastham, MA: Eastern National Park and Monument Association), 1988.

Selected Agencies

Appalachian Mountain Club
5 Joy Street
Boston, MA 02108
617-523-0636

Cape Cod National Seashore
South Wellfleet, MA 02663
508-249-3785

Massachusetts Audubon Society
South Great Road
Lincoln, MA 01773
617-259-9500

Massachusetts Department of Environmental
   Management
Division of Forests and Parks
100 Cambridge Street, 19th Floor
Boston, MA 02202
800-831-0569 (in Massachusetts); 617-727-3180

Massachusetts Division of Fisheries and Wildlife
508-792-7270

Metropolitan District Commission
20 Somerset Street
Boston, MA 02108
617-727-7090

Trustees of Reservations
527 Essex Street
Beverly, MA 01915-1530
508-921-1944

U.S. Fish and Wildlife Service
Northeast Region
300 West Gate Center
Hadley, MA 01035
413-252-8200

Index